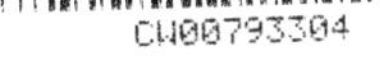

Birmingham Repertory Theatre Company and New Wolsey Theatre, Ipswich present

FEED THE BEAST

by Steve Thompson

Feed the Beast premiered in The STUDIO at Birmingham Repertory Theatre on 16 April 2015

FEED THE BEAST

by Steve Thompson

CAST

Kacey Ainsworth	Sally/Leader of the House of Commons
Gerald Kyd	Michael
Amy Marston	Heather/Curator of Chequers
Shaun Mason	Scott/Robert
Paul Moriarty	Chairman Denis/General Hume
Aimee Powell	Ellie
Badria Timimi	Andrea/Priscilla
Tristram Wymark	Clive/Anthony
	All other parts played by members of the company
Birmingham Supernumeraries	Brian Booth, Dina Dal Forno, Daisy Khera, James Millerin, Erin Quilliam, Nicholas Shelton, Bethany Westwood and Susan Winchcombe-Suggett
Ipswich Supernumeraries	Lucia Aguilar-Gomez, Maddy Caulfield, Rob Cook, Peter Edwards, Janice Leat, John Revell, Francis Thurstun-Crees and Katie Ward

CREATIVES

Peter Rowe	Director
Libby Watson	Designer
Simon Bond	Lighting Designer
Tom Mills	Composer and Sound Designer
Nathan Jones	Video Designer
Polly Jerrold	Casting Director
Nicholas Pitt	Assistant Director
Ruth Morgan	Company Manager
Jenny Campbell	Stage Manager
Bobbi McGlade	Deputy Stage Manager
Hannan Finnegan	Assistant Stage Manager

COMPANY

KACEY AINSWORTH

Sally/Leader of the House of Commons

Theatre credits include: *Loughton* (Stephen Joseph Theatre); *Calendar Girls* (National Theatre tour 2012); *Steel Magnolias* (Ambassadors Theatre Group); *Carrie's War* (Apollo, West End); *The Exonerated* (Riverside Studios); *Sleep With Me* (National Theatre); *The Taming of the Shrew* (English Touring Theatre); *Serving It Up* (Bush); *Pale Horse* (Royal Court Upstairs); *Attempts on Her Life* (Royal Court).

Television credits include: *Call the Midwife* Christmas Special, *Doctors*, *Casualty*, *The Wright Way*, *Holby Blue*, *Hotel Babylon*, *EastEnders*, *Happy Birthday Shakespeare*, *The Beggar Bride*, *Moonstone* (BBC); *Granchester*, *A Touch of Frost*, *Peak Practice III*, *Midsomer Murders* (ITV); *Touch and Go* (Arrowhead Productions/BBC).

Film credits include: *Topsy Turvey* (Thin Man Films); *That Lady from Rio* (Antena 3 TV/Casanova Pictures/Celtic Films).

GERALD KYD

Michael

Previous Birmingham Repertory Theatre credits include: *Ramayana*.

Theatre credits include: *Three Winters*, *Children of the Sun*, *The Cherry Orchard*, *Blood and Gifts* (National Theatre); *Richard III* (Trafalgar Studios); *Little Black Book* (Park); *55 Days*, *Revelation* (Hampstead); *The Real Thing* (West Yorkshire Playhouse); *The Years Between* (Royal Theatre Northampton); *This Much is True* (Theatre503); *The Seagull*, *Cyrano de Bergerac* (Royal Shakespeare Company); *The Three Musketeers* (Bristol Old Vic); *Conversations in Havana* (Òran Mór); *Edward II*, *Richard II* (Shakespeare's Globe); *Deathtrap* (P.W Productions); *Love's Labour's Lost* (English Touring Theatre); *Prophet in Exile* (Chelsea Centre); *The Local Stigmatic* (Lyric Studio, London).

Television credits include: *Sherlock*, *Casualty*, *Brief Encounters* (BBC); *The Bible* (History Channel); *The Midnight Beast* (Warp Films); *Persons Unknown* (Fox TV); *All in the Game* (Channel 4); *The New Professional*, *Underworld* (Hat Trick).

Film credits include: *Legacy* (Black Camel Pictures); *The Defender* (Lucky Seven); *Tomb Raider II* (Paramount); *Principles of Lust* (Channel 4).

AMY MARSTON

Heather/Curator of Chequers

Theatre credits include: *A Small Family Business*, *The Children's Hour* (National Theatre); *Stepping Out* (Salisbury Playhouse); *Man in the Middle* (Theatre503); *Don John* (BAC/Kneehigh); *Humble Boy* (Northampton Theatre Royal); *Enlightenment* (Abbey, Dublin); *After Mrs Rochester* (Shared Experience); *Henna Night*, *Sitting Pretty* (Chelsea Theatre); *Ghost Train Tattoo*, *Snake in a Fridge*, *Snapshots*, *Unidentified Human Remains* (Manchester Royal Exchange); *Eurydice* (Whitehall Theatre).

Television credits include: *DCI Banks* (Left Bank/ITV); *New Worlds* (Company Productions/Channel 4); *Frozen Addicts* (Wide Eyed Productions); *Unforgettable Amnesiac* (Dr Wide Eyed Productions); Toast (Ruby Films); *Consuming Passions*, *He Knew He Was Right*, *Judge John Deed*, *The Adventures of Tom Jones*, *Mrs Bradley Mysteries*, *Over Here*, *Between the Lines*, *Bottom* (BBC); *Rome* (HBO); *Jericho*, *Kingdom*, *The Last Detective* (ITV); *Man/Woman* (Talkback Productions);

Doc Martin (Buffalo); *The Final Quest*, *Heartbeat*, *The Black Velvet Band* (Yorkshire TV); *Where the Heart Is* (Anglia TV); *Hello Girls* (BBC/Feelgood Fiction); *Neverwhere* (Crucial Films).

Film credits include: *Personal Jesus* (El Nino); *Bel Ami* (Redwave Films); *The Imaginarium of Doctor Parnassus* (Poo Poo Picture Productions); *The Mascot* (Eclectic Films); *Charlotte Gray* (Ecosse Films).

Radio credits include: *Mr Spectator* (BBC Radio 4); *The Number of the Dead* (BBC Radio 3); *The Problem with Caves*, *The Running Lady*, *Couples*, *David Copperfield*, *Mr Fielding's Scandal Shop*, *The Glass Wright* (BBC Radio).

SHAUN MASON
Scott/Robert

Theatre credits include: *Peter Pan*, *Cinderella* (Liverpool Empire); *Macbeth*, *Billy Wonderful* (Liverpool Everyman); *Clockwork Orange* (Glasgow Citizens); *Macbeth*, *A Midsummer Night's Dream*, *Council Depot Blues*, *Stags and Hens* (Royal Court, Liverpool); *Sink or Swim* (Spike); *In Wonderland*, *Bright Phoenix*, *Tiny Volcanoes* (Everyword Festival); *Grotesque Chaos* (Nabakov); *Snow White*, *4 Girls and a Caravan*, *Night Collar*, *Cinderella*, *The Salon*, *Aladdin* (St Helens Theatre Royal); *When I Wake Up I Want to be Famous* (Fuse); *Blackberry Troutface* (Twenty Stories High); *Gods' Gift*, *King of Edge Hill*, *Your Breath in the Air*, *Of Mice and Men* (Unity, Liverpool).

Television credits include: *Cilla* (ITV); *Luther*, *Good Cop*, *Line of Duty* (BBC); *Moving On* (LA Productions); *Scott and Bailey* (Red Productions/Granada TV); *The Accused* (RSJ Films); *Shameless*,
3 Minute Wonder (Channel 4); *Brookside* (Mersey TV).

Film credits include: *Kelly and Victor* (Hot Property Films); *Fifteen Minutes That Shook the World* (Northstar Productions); *The Crew* (Adrian Vitoria); *Death Defying Acts* (Zephyr Films); *Revenger's Tragedy* (Exterminating Angel); *The Pool*, *3 Minute Wonder* (Channel 4).

Shaun was recently a member of the BBC Radio Drama Company, his credits include: *Take Me to Hope Street*, *As You Like It*, *The Once and Future King*, *Christmas Carol*, *A Steal*, *The Sound of Roses*, *For Whom the Bell Tolls*, *The Hot Kid*, *Love Songs of Miss Queenie Hennessy*, *The Rivals*, *Havana Quartet*.

Shaun has also worked on new writing development with Manchester Royal Exchange Theatre, Paines Plough and Liverpool Everyman and Playhouse Theatres.

PAUL MORIARTY
Chairman Denis/General Hume

Theatre credits include: *People*, *Market Boy*, *Pillars of the Community*, *Sing Yer Heart Out for the Lads*, *Macbeth*, *Black Snow*, *Murderers*, *As I Lay Dying*, *The Crucible*, *Racing Demon*, *Murmuring Judges*, *The Absence of War* (National Theatre); *King Lear*, *Penny for a Song*, *Antony and Cleopatra*, *Troilus and Cressida*, *Bingo*, *Dingo*, *Captain Swing*, *Twelfth Night*, *The Tempest* (Royal Shakespeare Company); *Translations* (Leicester Curve); *Nineteen Eighty-Four*, *Love and Money* (Young Vic/ Royal Exchange, Manchester); *Sus* (Young Vic); *Rosmerholm*, *Richard II*, *Coriolanus* (Almeida); *The Elephant Man* (Sheffield Lyceum/tour); *Saved* (Abbey, Dublin); *Afterbirth* (Arcola); *Kingfisher Blue* (Bush); *The Contractor* (Oxford Stage Company); *All My Sons* (Mercury, Colchester); *A View from the Bridge* (Sheffield Crucible); *Fool for Love* (English Touring Theatre); *Oi For England*, *Elizabeth I* (Royal Court); *The Mysteries* (Edinburgh Lyceum); *Serious Money* (Broadway); *Taking Part* (West End).

Television credits include: *WPC 56*, *Doctors*, *Holby City*, *Jack of Hearts*, *EastEnders*, *Pride and Prejudice*, *Between the Lines* (BBC); *Doc Martin* (Buffalo Pictures); *Ashes to Ashes* (Kudos); *A Touch of Frost* (Yorkshire TV); *The Knock*, *The Gentle Touch* (London Weekend TV); *Murder Most Horrid* (Talkback Productions); *Peak Practice* (Central Television); *Wycliffe* (HTV); *Maigret* (Granada Television); *The Comic Strip Presents* (Keith Allen); *Shine on Harvey Moon* (ITV); *Troilus and Cressida* (Jonathan Miller); *Saracens* (Herbie Wise); *South of the Border* (Antonia Bird); *The Bill* (Talkback Thames); *Paradise Club*, *Minder* (Euston Films); *The Sweeney* (Euston Films/Thames Television).

Film credits include: *Hidden Agenda* (Ken Loach).

AIMEE POWELL
Ellie

Aimee trained at Birmingham Theatre School.

Theatre credits include: *Macbeth* (Heartbreak Productions); *The Salvagers* (Tin Box Theatre Company); *Arabian Nights* (Blue Orange Arts); *Brighton Beach Scumbags*, *Dracula*, *Macbeth*, *The Elephant Man*, *Bed*, *Cathy Come Home* (Birmingham Theatre School); *Us and Them* (Letters to Eric Theatre Company).

Film credits include: *Music Room* (Lockwood Films); *A Dream I Had* (Short Night Films – winner of best short drama at the Isle of Wight Film Festival).

Aimee was named the winner of Monologue Slam at Birmingham Repertory Theatre in 2014.

BADRIA TIMIMI
Andrea/Priscilla

Badria trained at Bristol Old Vic Theatre School.

Theatre credits include: *Titus Andronicus*, *A Mad World, My Masters*, *Candide* (Royal Shakespeare Company); *The House of Bernarda Alba* (Almeida); *Tales from the Harrow Road* (Soho); *Birth of a Nation* (Royal Court); *The War Next Door* (Tricycle); *The Eleventh Minute* (Royal Court); *1001 Nights Now* (Northern Stage).

Television credits include: *Hollyoaks* (Lime Pictures); *DCI Banks* (Left Bank Pictures for ITV); *Killing Jesus* (National Geographic/Scott Free); *Drifters II* (Bwark Productions); *Whitechapel IV* (Carnival Film & Television); *Law & Order* (Kudos for ITV); *The Shadow Line* (Company Pictures); *The Little House* (ITV); *Doctors*, *Holby City*, *Silent Witness*, *The Grid*, *Messiah III*, *Walking with Cavemen*, *Casualty* (BBC); *The Fixer* (Kudos); *Generation Kill* (Company Pictures); *The House of Saddam* (BBC TV/HBO); *The Bill* (Fremantle); *Trial and Retribution* (La Plante Prods); *Prime Suspect*, *Secret Smile*, *Cold Feet* (Granada); *Afterlife* (ITV); *Murder Prevention* (World Productions Ltd); *Spooks* (Kudos).

Film credits include: *Syriana* (Warner Bros); *Pusher* (Pusher Productions).

Radio credits include: *Mr Acoustic Tries to Fall in Love*, *On the Rob*, *One Night in Winter*, *Promenade Rock*, *City of Victory*, *The Interview*, *Immigration Stories*, *The Eleventh Minute*, *Baghdad Burning* (BBC Radio).

TRISTRAM WYMARK
Clive/Anthony

Tristram trained at Central School of Speech and Drama.

Previous Birmingham Repertory Theatre credits include: *Anna's Room*, *Hamlet*, *Lady Windermere's Fan*.

Theatre credits include: *This May Hurt A Bit* (Out of Joint); *Cause Célèbre* (Old Vic); *Pygmalion* (Chichester Festival Theatre); *David Copperfield* (Mercury); *The Fastest Clock in the Universe* (Naach Theatre); *Nothing* (East 57th St Theatre); *David Copperfield* (West Yorkshire Playhouse); *Hamlet* (Barbican/Thelma Holt No1 Tour); *The Tempest* (Barbican/Thelma Holt No1 tour); *Semi-Munde* (Lyric); *Lady Windermere's Fan* (Apollo); *A Midsummer Night's Dream* (New Shakespeare Company); *The Collaborators*, *Phedre*, *Much Ado About Nothing*, *Richard III*, *Anna's Room*, *The Duchess of Malfi*, *The Critic* (National Theatre); *The Wild Sargasso Sea*, *The Tempest*, *The Cherry Orchard*, *Dance of Death*, *Mozart's Nachtmusik*, *Two Way Mirror*, *Pal Joey*, *Macbeth*, *The Millionairess*, *Widower's House*, *Hamlet*, *The Bar of a Tokyo Hotel*, *'Tis Pity She's a Whore*, *Phaedra*, *A Tale of Two Cities*, *Enrico IV*, *Mrs Warren's Profession* (Glasgow Citizens).

Television credits include: *Lucan* (ITV); *Call the Midwife*, *EastEnders Nuclear Race*, *Thin Air*, *Victoria Wood Play*, *Mrs Warren's Profession* (BBC); *Midsomer Murders* (Bentley Productions); *Getting Out Alive* (Raw Television); *Hollyoaks* (Lime Productions); *Joe's Palace* (Talkback Thames/BBC); *Hustle* (Kudos); *Ghost Ship* (Yorkshire Television); *Kavanagh QC* (Central Television); *Sharpe* (Carlton); *Jenny's War* (HTV); *Haggard* (Yorkshire Television).

Film credits include: *The Black Prince* (Brillstein Entertainment Partners); *The Cold Room* (Cold Room Productions); *Good and Bad at Games* (Portman Quintet Productions); *Another Country* (Castlezone Ltd).

CREATIVES

STEVE THOMPSON

Writer

Theatre credits include: *Damages* (Bush, Winner Arts Council Best New Play 2005); *Whipping It Up* (Bush/Ambassadors, Olivier nomination for Best New Comedy 2007); *Roaring Trade* (Paines Plough/Soho); *No Naughty Bits* (Hampstead).

Television credits include: *Sherlock* (BBC/Hartswood); *Doctor Who*, *Silk* (BBC).

He is married to the barrister Lorna Skinner and they live in Cambridge and Cornwall with their five children.

PETER ROWE

Director

After training at the Thorndike Theatre, Peter became the Artistic Director for the Southampton-based Solent People's Theatre and then Artistic Director for the London Bubble Theatre Company touring London in a big top tent. He has held two other Artistic Directorships, at the Gateway Theatre, Chester and the Liverpool Everyman, while freelance work has included productions for regional theatres and touring companies up and down the country. He has directed *Boyband* and *Return to the Forbidden Planet* in the West End and on national tours, together with his own musical, *Leader of the Pack.*

Peter is currently Artistic Director of the New Wolsey Theatre where his productions have included *Sweeney Todd*, *Perfect Days*, *Double Indemnity*, *A Family Affair*, *A Mad World, My Masters*, *Leader of the Pack*, *The Good Companions*, *Neville's Island*, Stephen Sondheim's *Company*, *Sugar*, *The Price*, *A Funny Thing Happened on the Way to the Forum*, *Vincent in Brixton*, *Blues in the Night*, *The Glass Menagerie*, *Laurel and Hardy*, *Little Shop of Horrors*, A *Chorus of Disapproval*, *Chimps*, a new musical adaptation of *It's a Wonderful Life*, *Noises Off*, *Up on the Roof*, *Guys and Dolls*, *Bedroom Farce*, *Mods and Rox*, *And Then the Dark*, the UK national tour of the Madness musical *Our House*, *Miss Nightingale*, a major revival of *The Threepenny Opera*, with co-director Jenny Sealey, and *Midsummer Songs.*

LIBBY WATSON

Designer

Libby trained at Bristol Old Vic Theatre School and Wimbledon School of Art.

Recent designs include: *Frankie and Johnny* (Chichester); *Fences* (Theatre Royal Bath/tou/West End); *Rudy's Rare Records* (Birmingham Repertory Theatre/Hackney Empire); *History Boys* (UK tour); *Propaganda Swing* (Belgrade/Nottingham Playhouse); *The Dead Dogs* (Print Room); *As You Like It* (Stafford Shakespeare Festival).

Future projects include: *Deranged Marriage* (UK tour); *Sweet Charity* (New Wolsey); *Lady Anna* (Park).

Other design credits include: *Twelfth Night* (Nottingham Playhouse); *One Monkey Don't Stop No Show* (Sheffield Crucible); *Bus Stop*, *A Fine Bright Day Today* (New Vic); *The Miser*, *Marriage*, *Stars in the Morning Sky*, *Babylone* (Belgrade Coventry); *Persuasion* (Salisbury); *God of Carnage* (Northampton); *Mountaintop* (Trafalgar Studios West End Winner of 2011 Lawrence Olivier Award for Best Play) *It's a Wonderful Life*, *Blues in the Night*, *Guys and Dolls* (Wolsey/tour);

Romeo and Juliet, *A Midsummer Night's Dream* (Stafford Festival); *Blonde Bombshells of 1943* (Hampstead); *Twelfth Night*, *Relatively Speaking*, *Three Men in a Boat*, *He's Much to Blame*, *Much Ado About Nothing*, *Dangerous Corner* (Bury St Edmunds Theatre Royal); *Far from the Madding Crowd* (English Touring Theatre); *Hello and Goodbye* (West End); *The French Lieutenant's Woman* (UK tour); *Up Against the Wall* (Octagon); *Christ of Coldharbour Lane* (Soho); *Macbeth* (Bristol Old Vic); *Under their Influence*, *Blues for Mr Charlie*, *Gem of the Ocean*, *Radio Golf* (Tricycle); *Crooked*, *I Like Mine With a Kiss* (Bush); *The Wills's Girls* (Tobacco Factory); *Blest Be the Tie*, *What's In the Cat* (Royal Court); *Man of Mode*, *Hysteria* (Northcott, Exeter); *Night of the Dons*, *Urban Afro Saxons*, *Sus*, *High Heeled Parrotfish* (Stratford East); *Hysteria*, *Respect*, *Three Sisters*, *Angel House* (Birmingham Repertory Theatre).

SIMON BOND
Lighting Designer

Simon is a Lighting Technician at Birmingham Repertory Theatre.

Lighting designs for Birmingham Repertory Theatre include: *Back Down*, *The Honey Man*, *Of Mice and Men*, *Never Try This at Home*, *Finger Trigger Bullet Gun*, *Circles*, *Come Heavy Sleep*, *Hopelessly Devoted*, *The Legend of Mike Smith*, *Europa*, *Wounded*, *Hip Hope Hero*, *Cling To Me Like Ivy*, *Gravity*, *Looking For Yogurt*, *The Just Price of Flowers* and *Notes to Future Self.*

For Birmingham School of Acting: *The Duchess of Malfi*, *Cloud 9*, *Hayfever*, *Dracula*, *Hedda Gabler.*

For Custom Practice: *A Midsummer Night's Dream*, *As You Like It.*

For Pentabus Theatre: *White Open Spaces*, *Strawberry Fields.*

NATHAN JONES
Video Designer

An innovative digital artist offering a range of creative services, Nat Jones (AKA Soopanatural) recently worked as Video Designer on *Khandan*, a co-production between Birmingham Repertory Theatre and the Royal Court Theatre in London. In addition, he was Video Designer for The Hip Hop Shakespeare Company's production of *Richard II* which was presented at the Southbank Centre in March, and created the digital environment for *The Legend of Mike Smith*, Soweto Kinch's theatre production which was directed by Jonzi D.

Soopanatural's artistic collaborations have included working with Nike, Soweto Kinch, Jonzi D, Akala, Charlie Dark, the Hip Hop Shakespeare Company, Mark De Clive-Lowe, Boy Blue Entertainment, Brighton Hip Hop Festival and Nu Century Arts.

Soopanatural Productions' work has featured on BBC interactive, at the Royal Court Theatre, London's Queen Elizabeth Hall, Royal Festival Hall, the TATE gallery, Cargo in Shoreditch, XOYO, Rome Colisseum and numerous theatre venues, music festivals and clubs in Europe.

POLLY JERROLD
Casting Director

Prior to becoming a freelance casting director Polly worked as Casting Associate at the Royal Exchange Theatre for over five years where she worked on a wide range of productions, from the world premiere of Simon Stephens' *Punk Rock*, to a production of Bernstein's *Wonderful Town* that was performed in association with the Hallé Orchestra under Sir Mark Elder.

Previous work for Birmingham Repertory Theatre includes the premiere of Rachel De'lahay's *Circles* in a co-production with the Tricycle Theatre, Steven Camden aka Polar Bear's debut play *Back Down* and a new adaptation of *A Christmas Carol* by Bryony Lavery, all with Tessa Walker directing.

Polly has just finished casting *Peter Pan* for Regent's Park Open Air Theatre with Timothy Sheader and Liam Steel directing and *The Ghost Train* for Told by an Idiot at the Royal Exchange.

Other recent work includes *James and the Giant Peach* for West Yorkshire Playhouse; a new musical version of *Rumpelstiltskin* at the egg at Theatre Royal Bath; Ella Hickson's *Merlin* for the Royal and Derngate and *Little Shop of Horrors* at the Royal Exchange.

Polly will shortly be working with The REP again on *Anita and Me*, with Roxana Silbert directing, and *The Lion the Witch and the Wardrobe* with Tessa Walker.

TOM MILLS

Composer and Sound Designer

Tom is a composer and sound designer for theatre and film.

Theatre credits include: *Death of a Comedian* (Lyric Belfast/Abbey/Soho); *Strike* (Turtle Key Arts); *Romeo and Juliet* (Tobacco Factory Bristol); *Dirty Butterfly*, *Far Away*, *A Streetcar Named Desire*, *Electra* (Young Vic); *The Importance of Being Earnest* (West End/tour); *Birdland*, *A Time to Reap* (Royal Court); *The Taming of the Shrew*, *Titus Andronicus* (Royal Shakespeare Company); *Enjoy* (West Yorkshire Playhouse); *The Way of the World*, *Benefactors* (Sheffield Crucible); *The Night Before Christmas*, *Pastoral*, *The Boy Who Fell Into a Book*, *Utopia*, *Realism*, *Mongrel Island* (Soho); *King Lear* (Theatre Royal Bath); *Bottleneck*, *Clockwork*, *Dusk Rings a Bell*, *Ditch*, *Lidless*, *Moscow Live* (Hightide); *Rock Pool*, *Top Secret* (Inspector Sands); *Cinderella*, *Aladdin*, *Dick Whittington* (Lyric Hammersmith); *Macbeth*, *Pericles* (Regent's Park); *The Alchemist* (Liverpool Playhouse); *Medea*, *Boys*, *A Midsummer Night's Dream*, *Edward Gant's Amazing Feats of Loneliness* (Headlong); *Purple Heart*, *Wittenberg*, *Breathing Irregular*, *The Kreutzer Sonata*, *Unbroken* (Gate); *The Dark at the Top of the Stairs* (Belgrade, Coventry).

NICHOLAS PITT

Assistant Director

Nicholas Pitt studied Drama at the University of Bristol, where he received the Vice Chancellor Warren Scholarship and is currently training on the prestigious Birkbeck Theatre Directing MFA.

He has worked as assistant director to Paulette Randall on Danny Robin's and Lenny Henry's *Rudy's Rare Records*, Roxana Silbert on John Steinbeck's *Of Mice and Men* and Nick Walker on Stephanie Riding's *Unknown Male* all at Birmingham Repertory Theatre.

Nicholas is also a long-term artistic associate with Idle Motion Theatre Company who, working with the British Council, have toured their original work to Europe, the Middle East and East Asia.

Credits with Idle Motion include: *Shooting With Light* (2015); *That is All You Need to Know* (2013); *Borges & I* (2012); *The Seagull Effect* (2011); *The Vanishing Horizon* (2010). Nicholas will next be working as assistant director to Michael Vale on the upcoming production of Geoff Thompson's *The Pyramid Texts* at Birmingham Repertory Theatre.

ABOUT BIRMINGHAM REPERTORY THEATRE

Birmingham Repertory Theatre is one of Britain's leading producing theatre companies. Founded in 1913 by Sir Barry Jackson, Birmingham Repertory Theatre Company rapidly became one of the most famous and exciting theatre companies in the country launching the careers of an array of many great British actors including Laurence Olivier, Ralph Richardson, Edith Evans, Paul Scofield, Derek Jacobi, Elizabeth Spriggs, Albert Finney and many more. In 2013 the company celebrated its centenary. Birmingham Repertory Theatre (The REP) is a local theatre with an international reach, acting as a cultural hub in the centre of Birmingham with the mission to create a vibrant programme of performance work that enriches the lives of the wide range of communities we serve and inspires artists to make their best work with us. As well as presenting over 60 productions on its three stages every year, the theatre tours its productions nationally and internationally, showcasing theatre made in Birmingham.

The commissioning and production of new work lies at the core of The REP's programme and over the last 15 years the company has produced more than 130 new plays. The theatre's outreach programme is the best of any cultural organisation in the city and engages over 25,000 young people every year. The REP is also committed to nurturing new talent through its youth theatre groups and training for up and coming writers, directors and artists.

Many of The REP's productions go on to have lives beyond Birmingham transferring to the West End and touring nationally and internationally. The REP's long-running production of *The Snowman* has become a must-see fixture in London's West End calendar, playing to packed houses at the Peacock Theatre every Christmas for the last 17 years. *The Snowman* also tours regularly across the UK and to theatres in Holland, Korea, Japan and Finland. Other transfers and recent tours include *Twelve Angry Men, Harvey, The King's Speech,* Kate Tempest's *Hopelessly Devoted,* Rachel De-lahay's *Circles and* Steve Camden's *Back Down.*

Artistic Director Roxana Silbert
Executive Director Stuart Rogers
Box Office 0121 236 4455
Administration 0121 245 2000
birmingham-rep.co.uk

Birmingham Repertory Theatre is a registered charity, number 223660

Birmingham Repertory Theatre Company

REP Patrons
June Brown
Soweto Kinch
Josie Lawrence
Martin Shaw
David Suchet
Dame Janet Suzman
Mark Williams

Directors of Birmingham Repertory Theatre Limited
Johanne Clifton
Jacqui Francis
Guy Hemington
Cllr Narinder Kaur Kooner
Greg Lowson
Angela Maxwell (Chair)
Rajiv Nathwani
Paul Phedon
Cllr Gary Sambrook
Prof Michael Whitby

Executive Director
Stuart Rogers

Artistic Director
Roxana Silbert

Associate Directors
Steve Ball
Tessa Walker

Associate Producer
Nisha Modhwadia

Creative Producer
Jenny Smith

Casting Co-ordinator
Alison Solomon

Arts Team Assistant
Johanna Taylor

Assistant Director
Nick Pitt

Assistant Resident Director (Regional Theatre Young Director Scheme)
Daniel Bailey

Associate Artists
Caroline Horton
KILN Ensemble

Senior Script Reader
Clive Judd

Cultural Intern
Lynette Dakin

Head of Learning and Participation
Michael O'Hara

Learning & Participation Manager
Lauren Fallon

Early Years Officer Telford
Kathryn Danby
Alison Hanson (Maternity Cover)

Education Officers
Fiona King
Holly Bateman (Maternity cover)
Mel Daly
Bhavik Parmar

Senior Youth Theatre Director
Tom Saunders

Youth Theatre Directors
Tom Mansfield
Daniel Tyler

Finance Director
Neil Harris

Financial Controller
Priya Pillalamarri

Finance Assistants
Sandra Bayliss
Christine Johnston
Claire Monk
Vidhu Sharma

General Manager
Trina Jones

Head of Marketing & Communications
Paul Reece

PR Manager
Clare Jepson-Homer
0121 245 2072

Campaigns Manager
Richard Leigh

Marketing Campaign Officers
Lucy Dwyer
Jess Wolinski

Publicity Assistant
Victoria Ellery-Jones

Business Development Manager
Anya Sampson

Sales Manager
Suzanna Barreiro Da Silva

Events Administrator
Triinu Uprus

Events Manager
Erika Jarvis

Banqueting & Events Supervisor
Vanessa Bernard

Business Development Officers
Rachel Cranny
Alana Tomlin

Theatre Sales Manager
Gerard Swift

Assistant Theatre & Sales Managers
James Dakers
Rachel Foster
Kieran Johnson
Maria Kavalieros

Theatre & Sales Assistants
Anne Bower
Fran Esposito
Robert Flynn
Matt Jukes
Sebastian Maynard-Francis
Eileen Minnock
Carla Smith
Rhys Worgan

Events Catering Supplied By
Just Good Food

Theatre Operations Manager
Nigel Cairns

Theatre Cleaning Supervisors
Jane Browning
Suri Matoo

Theatre Cleaning Assistants
Neville Claxton
Debra Cuthill
Ilyas Fareed
Maggie Maguire
Rebecca McDonald
Naomi Minnen
Tracey O'Dell
Doyle Cole

Head of Production
Tomas Wright

Production Manager
Milorad Žakula

Production Assistant
Laura Killeen

Company Manager
Ruth Morgan

Head of Wardrobe
Sue Nightingale

Costume Cutters & Makers
Fiona Mills
Kay Wilton

Head of Lighting
Andrew Fidgeon

Senior Technician (Lighting)
Simon Bond

Technician (Lighting)
Liam Jones

Head of Sound & AV
Dan Hoole

Senior Technician (Sound & AV)
Clive Meldrum

Head Scenic Artist
Christopher Tait

Design Manager
Olly Shapley

Head of Scenery & Props
Margaret Rees

Senior Scenic Maker
Simon Fox

Scenic Makers
Laura Davies
Amy Passey

Technical Co-ordinator
Adrian Bradley

Senior Technician (Events)
Alex Hughes

Building Maintenance Technician
Leon Gatenby

Technician (Stage)
Ross Gallagher

With thanks to all our Front of House Theatre Assistants, Stage Crew and Volunteers

Marmalade Bar and Bistro
0121 245 2080

ABOUT NEW WOLSEY THEATRE, IPSWICH

The New Wolsey Theatre is a 400 seat regional theatre with a national reputation for the quality, range and reach of its work and for embracing cultural diversity in the widest sense. It is central to the creative life of Suffolk and seeks to expand the horizons of audiences and artists by presenting a programme designed to entertain, enrich and challenge.

Nationally renowned for its producing work, both as a sole producer and in collaboration with a diverse range of UK artists and companies, the New Wolsey has a particular reputation for musical work, often employing actor-musicians. It is increasingly acknowledged as a leading player in the development of new musicals staging the world premieres of *It's A Wonderful Life*, *20th Century Boy* and *Mods & Rox*. In 2013, they produced a national tour of the Tim Firth and Madness musical *Our House*, using the same actor-musician formation, and have recently co-produced Brecht and Weill's *The Threepenny Opera* alongside Graeae Theatre Company, Nottingham Playhouse, Birmingham Repertory Theatre and West Yorkshire Playhouse.

The development of new talent is a priority for the New Wolsey and the annual PULSE Festival acts as a spring-board for fresh new artistic voices, as well as providing a home for risk-taking and cutting-edge performance from more established artists.

Alongside its work on stage, the New Wolsey runs an extensive Creative Learning programme which aims to provide opportunities for individuals to access innovative high quality arts provision and develop their creative, personal and social skills.

The New Wolsey Theatre has a proven track record of championing disabled led theatre and has launched 'Agent for Change' an initiative to create a freelance post to extend its engagement with disability arts and artists in the eastern region and to provide a support network for artists and arts organisations.

The New Wolsey received the 2012 TMA award for Most Welcoming Theatre, and was nominated as The Stage Award's Regional Theatre of the Year 2014. As a not-for-profit organisation and a registered charity, they rely on a variety of incomes streams such as part funding from the Arts Council, Suffolk County Council and Ipswich Borough Council as well as donations, individual giving and corporate support; all of which are invaluable.

Chief Executive **Sarah Holmes**
Artistic Director **Peter Rowe**

Box Office 01473 295900
www.wolseytheatre.co.uk

New Wolsey Theatre Staff List

BOARD OF DIRECTORS
Emma Champion, David Clements, Bonnie Collins, Adrian Grady, Isobel Hawson, Richard Lister (Chairman), Barbara Peirson, Louise Rogers, Hannah Skeates, Chris Waters

Chief Executive
Sarah Holmes

ARTISTIC
Artistic Director
Peter Rowe
Associate Director
Rob Salmon
Children's Shows Adviser
Adrian Berry
Agent For Change
Amy Nettleton
Agent For Change
Jamie Beddard

ARTISTIC ASSOCIATES
China Plate
Zoe Svensden
Paulette Randall

ADMINISTRATION
Head of Operations
David Watson
Finance & It Manager
Klyde Robinson
Administration & Human Resources Manager Lorna Owen
Finance Officer
Suzanne Simpson
Finance Officer
Terri Winwood
Administration Apprentice
Kirsten Day

BUILDING MAINTENANCE
Caretaker
Neil Daines
Cleaner
Keith Mickleburgh
Cleaner
Scott Mickleburgh

CREATIVE LEARNING
Creative Associate (Learning)
Sian Thomas
Creative Learning Administrator
Marcus Neal
Youth Theatre Leader
Helen Baggett
Drama Club Leader
Joe Leat
Youth Theatre Squared Leader
Tanya White

Youth Theatre Assistants
Tom Chamberlain, Debbie Grant, Liam Gregory, Mae Munuo, Jack Tricker, Ollie Ward

Youth Arts Practitioners
Liam Gregory, Amy Nettleton

Young Associates
Tom Chamberlain, Gemma Raw, Sam Rhodes, Jack Tricker

Freelance Practitioners
Helen Baggett, Mark Curtis, Danusia Iwaszko, Joe Leat

SALES AND MARKETING
Head of Sales and Marketing
Stephen Skrypec
Deputy Sales Manager
Michael Glasper
Press and Marketing Officer
Jeni Raw
Development and Marketing Officer
Elise Golbourn
Online Marketing Officer
Daniel Emmens
Digital Marketing Officer
Joseph Valentine
Outreach Officer
John Adam Baker

Ticket Sales Assistants
Lorna Garside, Jack Tricker, Jack O'Dell

PRODUCTION TEAM
Company Stage Manager
Tracey J Cooper
Technical Stage Manager
Julian Smith
Production Administrator
Zoe Double
Theatre Technician (Stage)
Matthew Ramsey
Theatre Technician (Lighting)
David Gardener
Theatre Technician (Sound)
Peter Hazelwood
Stage Management Apprentice
Alice Levey
Technical Apprentice
Aiden Standish

Production Casual Staff
Ben Ager, Elizabeth Gill Beckett, Matt Brand, James Cook, Steph Coxall, Dominic Eddington, Chris Flagg, Ronnie Green, Sam Hall, Roxy Last, Giles King, Callum Macdonald, Carolyn Nichols, Bill Parkin, Joanne Sebastian Groen, Danuta Tarbard, Jonathan Terry, Kyle Watts, Emily Watson

FRONT OF HOUSE
Front of House and Access Manager
Kelly Kirkbride
Deputy Front of House Manager
Jessica Baker
Catering and Bar Manager
Lauren Crowley
Deputy Catering and Bar Manager
Lianne Willis
Catering and Bar Supervisor
Kirstine Heald
Bar Supervisor
Cathy Hearne
Bar Supervisor
Lorna Garside

Front of House Assistants
Lucy Allen, Sally Appleby, Juliette Aktins, Sam Biscoe, Karina Brown, Charlotte Burtle, Sally Burtle, Stuart Cheadle, Eleanor Dodwell, Joshua Dowsing, Caroline Gould, Marcell Grant, Jordan Hales, Daniel Moore, Rebecca Pittway, Abigail Skrypec, Helen Taylor, Jack Tricker, Lauren Walker, Oliver Waters, Grace Wellfare.

Volunteer Ushers
Susan Andrews, Janet Black, Margaret Brown, Chris Bull, David Burgess, Rod Burrows, Tracey Cory, Clare Cotterill, Trevor Cowans, Maxine Darlow, Sandy Davies, Hugh Durrant, Yvonne Ellam, Jane Flack, Eric Fuller, Gerry George, Pat George, Anne Godbold, Peter Haffenden, Ben Horrex, Sonia Jackson, Dawn Mccracken, Mollie Markwell, Ron Markwell, Rena Mayoff, Alison Milne, Siobhan Moloney, Peter Mornard, Chris Mullard, Vicky Pannell, Janet Peacy, Pam Pelling, Ken Petherbridge, Debbie Reeve, Annie Ryall, Jo Shackleton, Steven Shaw, Carol Snell, Robert Snell, Sue Spencer, Ben Starling, Julie Stevenson, Tony Stevenson, Margaret Tilloston, Sarah Todd, Kirsty Torr, Samuel Turland, David Vince, Judy Wadman, Janice Waspe, Jackie Wells, Christopher White, Hazel Wilding, Julia Williamson, Leigh Williamson, Will Woolsgrove.

For more information on how you could get involved as a volunteer usher, please contact Jess Baker on jbaker@wolseytheatre.co.uk

Volunteer Ambassadors
Helen Charters, David Farthing, Vera Forsdike, Rachel Gowers, Jill Grosvenor, Sue Hall, Gary Kenworthy, Ellen Kirkby, Ruth Longhurst

Friday Club
Susan Abbott, Maureen Bailey, Joyce Bradley, Josephine Boggis, Lynn Cowling, Mervin Cunliffe, Mary Fuller, Eric Fuller, Heather Haines, June Jenkinson, Jean Johnson, Jean Legg, Jean Lockie, Robin Morrow, Pearl Nichols, Chloe Quantrill, Jean Roper, Christine Spall, Lewis Tyler, Kylie Welham, Margaret Woollard

For more information on how you could get involved as a volunteer ambassador or a member of the Friday Club, please contact John Adam Baker on jadambaker@wolseytheatre.co.uk

FEED THE BEAST

Steve Thompson

For Matt, who likes to talk politics
And for Moses, who doesn't

‘Today’s media is like a feral beast, tearing people and reputations to bits.’

Prime Minister Tony Blair

‘Feed the beast or it will bite you.’

James Carville,
Bill Clinton’s campaign manager

Characters

MICHAEL, *British Prime Minister*

ANDREA, *his wife*
ELLIE, *his daughter*

SALLY, *Chief of Staff*
SCOTT, *Press Officer*

DENIS, *Party Chairman*
CLIVE, *Chancellor of the Exchequer*
ROBERT, *Minister for Culture, Media and Sport*
PRISCILLA, *Minister for Education*

GENERAL SIR ALASTAIR HUME, *Chief of the Defence Staff*

HEATHER, *a newspaper executive*

ANTHONY, *new Chief of Staff*

THE LEADER OF THE HOUSE OF COMMONS
THE CURATOR OF CHEQUERS
A DIARY SECRETARY

MILITARY OFFICERS
PARTY GUESTS
POLITICAL ADVISERS
STEWARDS

All parts should be doubled, except for Michael.

This text went to press before the end of rehearsals and so may differ slightly from the play as performed.

ACT ONE

Scene One

10 Downing Street. The private study.

Pale walls, antique furniture, sash windows. Two doors.

Bright light of morning.

MICHAEL *stares out of the window, watches the street below. Sounds of London.*

Sharp knock. Door opens. CLIVE *enters, the Chancellor of the Exchequer.*

MICHAEL. Clive.

CLIVE. Prime Minister.

They shake hands cordially.

Can I be the first to say it? 'Well done.' So delighted.

MICHAEL. Thank you. (*Breath.*) What about?

CLIVE (*'Isn't it obvious?'*). You won.

Beat.

MICHAEL. You're delighted?

CLIVE. Yes. (*Beat.*) Don't I seem it?

MICHAEL. No, you do. You *seem* it. And you *are*. The two don't necessarily follow.

CLIVE (*laughs*). Ah.

MICHAEL. You're not the first, though.

CLIVE. 'The first'?

MICHAEL. To congratulate me.

CLIVE. Busy day for you.

MICHAEL. Packed.

CLIVE. Assembling a Cabinet.

MICHAEL. Chocka.

CLIVE. Meeting the team. Stroking the talent.

MICHAEL. Like the dinner party from hell. 'Where do I put everyone?' (*Beat. Smiles.*) You brought a letter?

CLIVE. I… (*Baffled.*) A letter?

MICHAEL. Resignation.

Long beat.

CLIVE. You want me to resign?

MICHAEL. It'll save you some embarrassment, later on.

Beat.

CLIVE. I'm confused.

MICHAEL. Get in there quick. Jump before you're pushed. Tell the press we couldn't rub along.

Pause.

CLIVE. You're firing me?

MICHAEL. Not if you resign.

Beat.

CLIVE. You're firing me.

MICHAEL. Yep. Can we move the conversation on?

CLIVE. This is about the leadership contest. (*Beat.*) Because I… threw my weight behind the other man. (*Beat.*) We all *said things*. During the campaign. Surely… this is… (*Can't find the words.*)

MICHAEL. 'A time for Party unity'?

CLIVE. Exactly.

MICHAEL. Nope. This is a time for you to piss off, I think. I can lend you some paper if you want to dash off that note.

CLIVE (*rallying*). It'll look like churlishness.

MICHAEL. Know what? It'll look like that because *I'm churlish*. Man gets called a truculent shit – usually means he's a truculent shit. No hidden depths in politics.

CLIVE. Look… I didn't support your campaign because I thought you… lacked… a certain… *sheen*.

MICHAEL. You're vindicated. Bravo. I lack a lot of things. 'Tolerance' for one. Chief of my failings: I CAN'T TOLERATE YOU.

CLIVE. Michael…

MICHAEL. I respect your hatred, Clive. You don't like me. Never have. Somehow I cope. What I can't stomach is the way you're pretending to adore me right now. Just to save yourself. Please, bugger off.

CLIVE (*blustering*). Four straight quarters of fiscal growth. I'm a success!!

MICHAEL. Lovely. How many push-ups can you do?

CLIVE. You can't afford to lose your best people.

MICHAEL. You're not *my people*. Never were.

CLIVE. Michael…

MICHAEL. No. I WON'T!! (*Beat.*) I won't do it. It would sicken me – the masquerade. Every Cabinet meeting, pretending you esteem me. *We are nothing unless we are ourselves*. Honesty is all. GO AND BE FREE. FREE TO HATE ME.

Scene fades…

Scene Two

Mid-morning.

MICHAEL *is with his Chief of Staff* (SALLY, *forties*) *and the Party Chairman* (DENIS, *fifties*).

Coffee served by the CHIEF STEWARD. MICHAEL *is woofing his way through a plate of biscuits, inescapably hungry.*

DENIS. Settling in?

MICHAEL. Oh, you know. Sort of. Grab what space you can. (*Gestures around.*) I bagsied this. (*Breath.*) Turns out there's no actual *office*.

DENIS. No.

MICHAEL. Like being a kid again. I used to fight with my brother to get the top bunk bed. (*Stares around.*) Wilson chose this room.

DENIS. Oh?

MICHAEL. Apparently. (*Points to the desk and chair.*) Sat there. Abolished the death penalty.

DENIS. He did.

MICHAEL. Invented social liberalism. Made 'bum sex' legal, sitting right there, on that cushion. (*Made himself laugh with the choice of phrase. Properly giggling.*) I mean can you imagine the conversation. Loved to have been a fly on the wall for that one. There's no statesmen-like language, is there? 'Gentlemen, I'm putting "bum sex" top of our agenda.'

His wife ANDREA *knocks and enters. Looks rather flustered.*

ANDREA. Sorry, sorry.

MICHAEL. No, come in.

ANDREA. Sorry to intrude.

MICHAEL. Is everything okay?

DENIS (*greeting her ebulliently*). Andrea.

ANDREA. Denis. Hello. (*For* MICHAEL.) Just popping out. Need furniture. For Ellie's room. Nothing here suitable for teenage kids, you know.

MICHAEL. You want me to come?

ANDREA. Aren't you… *governing*?

MICHAEL. Er… (*Making an assessment.*) Not yet. Let me come. We can find an Ikea.

ANDREA. She needs a duvet. And a desk. (*Catches* DENIS*'s expression.*) Stay. I'll get the guard to run me.

MICHAEL. Stop at a garage. Bring chocolate.

ANDREA. Right-oh.

Gives him a kiss and is gone. MICHAEL *nods at the door after she has disappeared.*

MICHAEL. Total bodge, whole bloody house.

DENIS. Oh?

MICHAEL. Pokey little bedrooms. But then a dining room you could land a plane in. Plus the kitchen's right down in the basement. Three flights every time I want a KitKat.

DENIS (*steering him back*). Anyway. This meeting.

MICHAEL (*not listening*). The thing I can't deal with is the loo.

An odd silence whilst they take this in.

How many famous backsides have touched down there? How many different ideologies. Freaks me out – sitting on the same seat as Thatcher. Feels wrong, somehow.

DENIS (*steering him back*). Same question again and again: 'Is he calling an election?'

SALLY. Mr Chairman…

DENIS. Taking over, mid-term.

MICHAEL. An election, eh?

DENIS. Be your own man. Don't spend the next two years in someone else's… what's the word?

MICHAEL. Majority.

DENIS. Shoes.

MICHAEL. Ah.

DENIS. I can organise the troops for you. The whole campaign. Put two hundred laptops in an office. We'll be ready to roll in a week. You say the word and we're 'Go go go'.

MICHAEL. I've only just sat down, Denis.

DENIS. Sure, but…

MICHAEL. Only just unpacked my pyjamas. Put my tin of pencils on the desk. You want me on the campaign trail. I've got things I want to do. Health Service is in a right old mess.

DENIS. This Party – it's a tree.

Beat. Then MICHAEL *bursts out laughing. Can't help it. Such an absurd image. He manages to rein it in.*

MICHAEL. Where are you going with this?

DENIS. Some years it withers, some years it thrives. We're in bloom right now, and you –

MICHAEL. I'm the highest bud. (*Finds this all terribly funny.*) That's where you're going with this.

DENIS. Yes.

MICHAEL. Okay. Up with your style.

DENIS. You've got roots – in the electorate, yes. But no… *foliage*. No cover. We don't… surround you.

MICHAEL. 'We.'

DENIS. The Party.

MICHAEL. Ah. So – this poncey tree metaphor… it's just a way of telling me I'm not popular. (*Beat.*) I'm not popular. With some of my colleagues.

DENIS. You have a style…

MICHAEL. Disarming.

DENIS. Honest.

MICHAEL. And it… might turn out to be an issue?

DENIS. Two years – you'll be forced to go to the polls. SEIZE THE MOMENT. Best chance you'll have. Before… (*Breath.*)

MICHAEL. What? What happens? (*A daft guess.*) I explode.

MICHAEL *raids the plate of biscuits again. A chance for his Chief of Staff to wade in.*

SALLY. Stuff to do in this country, Mr Chairman. Big thumping changes we need, to our hospitals, our schools.

DENIS. Sure…

SALLY. First one hundred days are when something actually gets done. Can't throw away our best moment.

MICHAEL *is on his feet, spouting his creed, mouth full of biscuit.*

MICHAEL. Everyone is sooo disengaged, Denis. Democracy is dead. Truly. Died in this country – long time ago. I want to make politics hip again.

DENIS. Super.

MICHAEL. Clean air, good schools. Stuff that should matter to everyone. A bricklayer – he goes to work and at the end of the day he comes home and there's *a wall*. I want to do that. I want to BUILD. Elections are – quite frankly – a major distraction.

DENIS. Okay, yes but…

MICHAEL. Fifty thousand more doctors, just for starters. A hundred thousand nurses. GPs available weekends. Free cancer prescriptions. Winter fuel allowance. Record maternity pay. Free nursery places. I want to triple overseas aid. I want peace in Northern Ireland cast in stone. Half a million kids dragged out of poverty. SHOPPING LIST OF SOCIAL CHANGE. (*Breath.*) Sorry. I spat biscuit on you. (*Beat as he brushes it off, apologetic smile.*) I didn't expect to *be here*, Denis. All a big surprise.

DENIS. Your competitors did split the vote.

MICHAEL. The outsider. 'Not PM material.' I'm not cuddly like my predecessor. Rough-hewn.

DENIS (*'Yes.'*). Well. If you say so.

MICHAEL. I understand your misgivings. You're sensing trouble up ahead. 'Once they get to know me they'll hate me.' You're saying I should win them over – before I've made a mess.

DENIS *opens his mouth to interrupt.*

You're thinking about your pension. Want to keep your job a little while longer. I can smell the fear.

DENIS. Yes, look…

MICHAEL. Why is everyone obsessed by the next election? It's like planning your funeral when you're a teenager. I have this… energy, Denis. A real hunger for change. We need a hundred thousand council homes.

DENIS. We do.

MICHAEL. I'm in a position to fix that. I won't give it up in order to go on the road!

Beat. DENIS *struggling to come on board.*

DENIS. Maybe… there *is* something to be gained from waiting. (*Points to chair.*) Your predecessor was terribly popular. So. Let's play the 'continuity' card. Finishing up his work.

MICHAEL. I'm the Prime Minister. Not the caretaker.

DENIS. Michael…

MICHAEL. 'Finishing up his work.' He was a waster!! A hairdo. No substance. Didn't follow through. Sing his praises in the street if you want. My eulogy for him is four words: 'Thank fuck he's scarpered.'

DENIS *swallows his surprise.*

Greatest office in the land – his big achievement was to change the Party logo. He got an award from *GQ*. Found it in the bogs. 'Best dressed politician.' Says EVERYTHING about the man.

DENIS. Michael, look…

MICHAEL. I'm not 'playing the legacy card' just to win favour. Nor am I rushing to the polls! I didn't come here just to seize the throne and then hang on for as long as is physically possible. Day one. Out of the traps. Start governing. Wham! HOW DO WE WANT TO SHAPE THIS LAND? Don't come in here and ask me to focus on 'how to string this out'. You're bloody belittling everyone.

Pause. MICHAEL *celebrates his speech by devouring a biscuit whole.*

It isn't just about winning.

DENIS (*unconvinced*). That's a very nice speech, but…

Door flies open. It's ANDREA.

MICHAEL. Not gone?

ANDREA. Can you help me measure her room?

MICHAEL *scuttles out after her, without a pause.*

SALLY *is left alone with* DENIS *momentarily.*

DENIS. He seems…

SALLY. Yes.

DENIS. …very eager.

SALLY. Bulldozer. Stuck in top gear. Exhilarating. It's why I came to work here.

Scene fades…

Scene Three

Evening.

Pink and orange sky.

MICHAEL *is showing his sixteen-year-old daughter around the office. First opportunity.* ELLIE *is an intelligent but rather gauche girl – oddly intense.*

MICHAEL. How's everything?

ELLIE. Oh dear. A talk.

MICHAEL. No, just… No. (*Beat.*) Everything all right? Not had a… chance. Not since we… you know.

ELLIE. *This is a talk.*

MICHAEL. I want to ask how you're doing. Do you want to try my chair? (*Breath.*) Nice chair. (*Dry.*) Spins round and everything.

Beat.

ELLIE. Are you being a dad now?

MICHAEL. Trying to be. You want to play along? You can pretend that you're a daughter.

ELLIE. Sure. Let's do it.

MICHAEL. Go out into Downing Street with a frisbee. Maybe have a run round on your scooter.

Laughter.

There is a newspaper on his desk. ELLIE *picks it up, glances.*

ELLIE (*reads the byline*). 'Dynamic energy at the dispatch box.'

MICHAEL. First Prime Minister's Questions.

ELLIE. Good start.

MICHAEL. Apparently so.

ELLIE. What did you do? To make everyone so impressed?

MICHAEL. I sang a karaoke set. Couple of Sinatra songs, you know.

She giggles.

I cut the defence budget.

ELLIE. Waydago.

MICHAEL. Cancelled a few missiles. Got us some dosh we badly need.

ELLIE. Gonna buy me a stunt bike with it?

MICHAEL. Hospitals building programme, actually. (*Beat.*) It's not hard to be a good guy. We should have the country back on its feet by… Friday teatime. You just have to be… unafraid.

ELLIE. Why do I feel as if this talk is about to get… meaningful?

Beat.

MICHAEL. Is everything going… okay?

Beat.

ELLIE. Who's the bloke? In the uniform? Walks up and down in the corridor?

MICHAEL. Chief Usher?

Beat. She blushes guiltily.

What did you do? (*Beat.*) Ellie?

ELLIE. I left yesterday's knickers and socks on the carpet.

Beat.

MICHAEL. Okay. That doesn't sound… too bad.

ELLIE. He made a little speech about princes and kings.

MICHAEL. Ah.

ELLIE. 'Princes and kings will walk through here.'

MICHAEL. He made you pick up your pants.

ELLIE. Will you sack him?

MICHAEL. Oh. Sure.

ELLIE. Whip him through the streets.

MICHAEL. Top of my agenda: bringing down the people who've been mean to you. Anything else, or is that it? I've got the nuclear launch codes round here somewhere.

Shared laughter.

Pats the chair next to him. She sits.

Do me a favour. Develop an edge.

ELLIE. What?

MICHAEL. Whilst we're here.

ELLIE (*gestures to the door*). He's annoying. His nose whistles when he talks.

MICHAEL. I don't mean him. I don't mean the Chief Usher. I'm the Prime Minister. Stuff is going to happen to us.

Beat.

ELLIE. Stuff? (*Beat. Guesses.*) People being mean. About my dad.

MICHAEL (*wields the newspaper, his success*). Every day won't be like this. I know how you get.

ELLIE. 'How I get.'

MICHAEL. Don't make this difficult. I'm saying there'll be days when I get criticised. It's important you stay off the internet.

ELLIE. You don't want me wigging out.

MICHAEL. I don't want you getting… anxious all over again. It's been good for you to repeat the year.

ELLIE. Maybe. (*Shrugs.*) My mates are all at sixth form now. (*Beat.*) Have I made things difficult?

MICHAEL. Don't. I bloody love you. You're great. You're my lass. (*A cuddle.*) We never talked about… you know. I never asked if you minded. Coming here. I know that you have a lot… of worries going on in there. (*Taps her forehead.*)

ELLIE. I worry about that usher bloke. He hates me.

MICHAEL. You should go. You got bus money?

ELLIE. No. I've got a car. Terry drives me. And Terry has a gun.

MICHAEL. Personal driver at sixteen.

ELLIE. I know. It totally rocks.

He opens his arms.

MICHAEL. No one's looking. One hug.

She hugs him warmly.

Scene fades…

Scene Four

Early morning.

SALLY *ushers in* ROBERT*, the Minister for Culture, Media and Sport. On the young side for a minister – thirties, groomed, dashing.*

But today he looks pale and wan, been through the mill.

ROBERT. Prime Minister.

MICHAEL. Robert.

They shake hands. SALLY *shuts the door.*

SALLY. It's going to break.

ROBERT. Shit. Shitbugger.

SALLY. Tomorrow. Maybe the weekend. Maybe the Sundays. Okay, this is painful. It's no fun picking over your private life…

MICHAEL (*mock-determination*). But dammit we're doing it anyway.

MICHAEL *and* SALLY *exchange a glance. She doesn't want him to be flippant about this.*

SALLY. My office got a call from a reporter. We need to be suited up.

ROBERT. Of course.

SALLY. Can you tell us what's occurred?

Beat. Difficult to say.

ROBERT. One of my staff. A researcher.

SALLY. Yes?

ROBERT. I sent some texts.

SALLY. We just need the headlines, Robert. Not a blow-by-blow.

MICHAEL *laughs at the saucy reference, then stifles it.*

MICHAEL. Sorry.

ROBERT. We've been seeing each other.

SALLY. 'Seeing.'

MICHAEL (*'It's obvious!'*). 'Seeing' is sex.

SALLY. Thanks, yes. I'd rather Robert talked us through.

ROBERT. He has a flat.

SALLY. 'He.'

ROBERT. Glenn.

MICHAEL (*rather jokey*). Oh shit, Robert! Please, please tell us he's not doing work experience.

ROBERT. He's twenty.

MICHAEL (*mock-relief, still jokey*). Phew. Twenty. That's the good news.

SALLY. Does your wife know?

ROBERT. We've spoken.

SALLY. Good. Good. So. Now it's just the press.

ROBERT. 'Just'?

SALLY. Can we guess the angle?

ROBERT. The angle is I'm having an affair.

SALLY. That's not enough for them. They can't call that public interest. Did you fail to do your job?

ROBERT. I wouldn't say so, no.

SALLY. Did you promote him? Pass him classified documents?

ROBERT *shakes his head.*

Did you allow him any sort of access to places where he… frankly… shouldn't have been?

MICHAEL *can't help it. This makes him laugh out loud.*

MICHAEL. Sorry. Sorry.

SALLY. What about expenses?

ROBERT. I've taken him on trips.

SALLY. Where he wasn't essential.

ROBERT. Possibly.

SALLY. Shit. Then that's the headline.

Beat. ROBERT *looks disconsolate.*

And… are you leaving Helen? (*Beat.*) Are you ending the affair? I'm sorry. This is awful. Feels like Special Branch.

ROBERT. I honestly don't know.

SALLY. You need to choose.

MICHAEL. What?

SALLY. That's how we change the story. 'Minister leaves wife.' Puts you in control.

ROBERT. You *want* me to leave my wife?

MICHAEL. She's not saying that.

SALLY. 'Minister ends affair.' That'll do just as well.

ROBERT. You're asking me to choose right now?

MICHAEL. No.

SALLY. End of the day.

ROBERT. Jesus.

MICHAEL*'s had enough. Slams his fist into the table.*

MICHAEL. Robert, could you leave us? We need to have a row.

And ROBERT *scuttles out.*

Silence.

SALLY. What?

MICHAEL. He's a person.

SALLY. I hadn't forgotten.

MICHAEL. He's a person. And his wife's a person too.

SALLY. I'm managing the situation.

MICHAEL (*dry*). Oh, thank God.

SALLY. You are making progress, Michael; you're doing your thing; you're turning this country around. Proper social issues – being addressed. We want the press writing THAT. Not sleazy little distractions.

MICHAEL. Sal…

SALLY. In office for less than a month. They're all desperately hoping we'll trip over ourselves. We have to handle this. We have to have a strategy. Or it will dominate the headlines and we'll be on the back foot.

MICHAEL. This meeting is about 'them'? The press?

SALLY. Of course!

MICHAEL. Right. And I thought we were counselling a colleague.

SALLY. He was given tea and a biscuit. Don't start with the moral outrage.

MICHAEL. Already there. Already feeling it!!

She looks at him and then her eyes go wide.

SALLY. Oh please oh don't. Don't make this into a *crusade*, Michael.

MICHAEL. Sal…

SALLY (*exasperation*). How long have we known each other? You'd really think I'd have got to know you by now. Turns out I don't. Turns out every bloody day I CAN'T… PREDICT WHAT YOU'RE GOING TO CARE ABOUT!!

MICHAEL. Sal…

SALLY. I signed up to be your Chief of Staff.

MICHAEL. I do recall.

SALLY. Left a six-figure salary.

MICHAEL. I never tire of being reminded.

SALLY. I left an office I had just decorated – bloody expensive wallpaper – left to run your administration. Because I'm a true believer, Michael. You're the real deal – unfettered by personal motives. You're here because you want to serve. Don't hand the press a reason to shift the focus.

MICHAEL. Sorry. Bad luck. *This* is what I'm doing. *This*. This is the very next thing that's ripe for change.

SALLY. You're going to take on the press?

MICHAEL. No. I'm going to ignore them.

SALLY. Michael, that's insane.

MICHAEL. Bloke put his knob in a young researcher. I assume that's what he did. I don't actually want to speculate. Only person it affects is his wife – but you're asking me to waste my time making sure some newspaper *isn't going to be mean*?

SALLY. It matters what 'they' think. Come on, Mike.

MICHAEL. It matters what they think in an election.

SALLY. It's always an election here!!

Beat.

MICHAEL. I don't want to comment. Nope. Won't comment.

SALLY. Michael…

MICHAEL. I refuse to spend my days here… REACTING.

SALLY. Okay. (*Breath.*) And… when we go down in a shitstorm?

MICHAEL. Let our legacy be… we wouldn't play their game.

SALLY. This is a joke!! Please tell me it's a wind-up. A dozen editors will eat this thing for breakfast, lunch and tea.

MICHAEL. And I'm saying let them do their worst. Let's not try to control it.

SALLY. Have you been eating sweets?

MICHAEL. Listen to me! I cannot bring myself to accept the highest office in the land and then trade only in gossip!! (*Pointing to his chair.*) I don't want to walk in *his* footsteps. I don't want to be that man. I have a country to run – *not* a story to contain. You're confusing me with – (*Gestures to the chair.*) that lightweight. One in four kiddies living in poverty – and I should devote this morning to a text of someone's privates? NO THANK YOU. THANK YOU – NO! I don't know how we've ended up here but it stops right now. We'll take some hits – sure. The press will have some fun. But they will not set the agenda. Not for me. And not for this Government. Now you go back out there and tell him his genital acts are not our purview.

SALLY. And… when the press begin their feeding frenzy?

MICHAEL. 'Mind your own bloody business.' That's the Downing Street you get to run.

Pause.

SALLY. We should have talked about this. (*Beat.*) I hate these moments.

MICHAEL. When I win.

SALLY. When you convince me. Mm.

MICHAEL. You know I'm right.

SALLY. You deserve to be right. We're going to have to make some changes.

MICHAEL. How exactly?

Scene fades…

Scene Five

Lunch meeting.

MICHAEL *and* SALLY *are interviewing* SCOTT, *a young Press Secretary.*

MICHAEL. I've got to be honest, Scott… it does sound like the sort of thing I would say.

SCOTT. 'Titting shitbag.'

MICHAEL. Definitely my style.

SALLY. You called him 'Titting shitbag'?

MICHAEL. Mm. First time we ever met.

SCOTT. It's stuck, as it happens, sir. I'm 'Titting Shitbag' to everyone. (*With wry humour.*) My mum, she says it too.

SALLY. Sorry. Remind me, would you please…? (*Doesn't know this story.*)

MICHAEL (*telling* SALLY). Back when I was Secretary of State for Employment… Treasury and I were at odds, they didn't want to finance my labour scheme. (*To* SCOTT.) You planted stories dissing me.

SCOTT. And you shouted 'Titting shitbag'. *At me.* Right across the lobby. (*Beat. Bit meekly.*) I was doing my job.

MICHAEL. Dissing me.

SCOTT (*shrugs: 'Of course.'*). I was Junior Press Secretary at the Treasury. If I'd known you were going to be Prime Minister, then obviously…

MICHAEL (*amused*). Obviously you wouldn't have rubbished me. (*Little laugh.*) Best thing about this job. Everyone who's ever been mean to you is feeling like a tosser now. There was a bloke at primary school who stole my Quavers… I expect he's emigrated, don't you?

Shared smile.

You're a fast-streamer. On his way up.

SCOTT (*shrugs*). Well…

MICHAEL. That's the gossip in The Westminster Arms these days.

SALLY. We need a new Press Officer.

SCOTT. What happened to the last one?

MICHAEL. We need a new one.

SCOTT. Why?

SALLY. Change of strategy.

Beat.

MICHAEL. We need to begin again. With a fresh face.

SCOTT. Okay. Uh-huh.

MICHAEL. Someone from the Civil Service.

SCOTT. Ah.

MICHAEL. *Not* a political appointee. Not a buddy. Not a crony.

SCOTT (*smiles, understands*). Nobody trusts an insider.

MICHAEL. Put your best pal on the podium to speak, well – frankly it looks bad. It makes the information seem…

SCOTT. 'Suspect'?

MICHAEL. Delivered by one of the cool kids.

SCOTT. Okay. So… I'm *not* one of the cool kids. Got it.

MICHAEL. You're new. Ish. And young. Ish.

SALLY. Not a face they would easily recognise.

MICHAEL. They won't beg favours from someone they don't know. We can build a whole new system from the ground again. (*Jumps up, spouting his theories.*) New rules. No media lunches. No leaks. No tip-offs. The press lobby is totally off-limits.

SCOTT. No press relationships… at all?

MICHAEL. No.

SCOTT (*murmurs*). Well. I can see why the last guy didn't stick it.

MICHAEL *is whirling around the room, spouting his new ideas, excited by them.*

MICHAEL. Above all – you get nothing from me that isn't policy-related. That's our creed. No personality pieces. No shots of me building snowmen with my kids.

SCOTT. I see. (*Beat.*) And the fact that you *hate me* just a little. The fact that you've been rude about me publicly…

MICHAEL. …adds to the sense you're not a crony.

SCOTT. 'Titting shitbag.'

MICHAEL. 'Titting shitbag.'

SCOTT. Right. With you.

SALLY *puts a newspaper in front of* SCOTT.

SALLY. You've seen the Cornell coverage? That stuff with his researcher…

SCOTT (*glances at it*). No statement from Number 10.

MICHAEL. Story died. Because we didn't feed it. That's the road we're taking. DON'T FEED THE BEAST. Are you in?

Beat.

SCOTT. 'Don't feed the beast'?

MICHAEL. I will talk about this office. I will talk about my vision till the mountains crumble into the sea. But I won't talk personalities. It isn't necessary for people to like me.

Pause. SCOTT *considering this extraordinary stance.*

SCOTT. Sorry, sorry. Hold on just a second. Sorry. Can we just rewind a little bit? It isn't necessary that people… *like you*???

MICHAEL. How many people are on friendly terms with their window cleaner?

SCOTT. With respect…

MICHAEL. How many people are intimate with their… bank manager?? Or their plumber?? This isn't a seduction routine. I'm not trying to take the country on a date. Judge me by my work. Not my choice of aftershave.

Beat.

SCOTT. It's a risky strategy.

MICHAEL (*'So what?'*). Yep.

SCOTT. I mean… a void gets filled. They have column inches to supply. You don't dish out enough juice: they go elsewhere. And if you don't brief – your competitors will provide.

MICHAEL. Just feed them policy policy policy. Political reporting the way it used to be. WE DON'T TRADE IN GOSSIP ANY MORE. If you want the job it's yours.

SCOTT. You're asking me to step off a cliff.

Beat.

SALLY. Questions? (*Beat.*) You must have questions.

Long beat.

SCOTT. Can I ask about hats?

Beat. Everyone slightly taken aback.

MICHAEL. I'm sorry?

SCOTT. You wear one?

MICHAEL (*'Where's this going?'*). Not… usually, no.

SCOTT. Baseball caps. Oh, and turbans. Turbans are a nightmare. Visiting the Far East, you sometimes get forced to wear one, don't you?

Beat.

MICHAEL. You're worried about… hats?

SCOTT. Ballroom dancing? Do you do any ballroom dancing?

MICHAEL. Not if I can help it, no.

SCOTT. What about eating overly large sandwiches? Ones where you have to… contort your mouth to choke the thing down.

SALLY. What's the point you're making here, Scott, hm?

SCOTT. Most of the voters out there will never actually meet you. The press is their only point of access. And the press can be *bribed* into a favourable view of you. But the press are…. out of bounds.

MICHAEL. Uh-huh.

SCOTT. I can't meet them. I can't *stroke* them. I can't *rub them up* under the restaurant table. All I can do is to point in your direction and say 'That is what you're getting.'

MICHAEL. You catch on fast. You're the man for this. Definitely.

Beat.

SCOTT. Sir, I watched you on TV last night, opening up that flagship hospital. Moseley. You stood in front of the plaque.

MICHAEL. What?

SCOTT. Balls-up. Total. The cameras couldn't film it.

MICHAEL. Er, I don't recall…

SCOTT. Tapped the microphone before you spoke. Actually tapped it to see if it was working. As if the PA guy had forgotten you were the most powerful man in the land and hadn't turned it on for you! You turned a speech by the leader of this nation into a… well… a sort of an apology. Tapping the end like a stand-up comic who's walked on for his very first gig. I cringed when I was watching.

SALLY. Scott…

SCOTT. These are all basic errors. Anyone in my job would be fired for letting you make them. But you're going to ignore the damage. AND GO ON IGNORING IT. Dream job. When do I begin?

Pause.

MICHAEL. You have an interesting personal style. Were you at all popular at the Treasury?

SCOTT. Actually, if they were calling me names I wasn't in the room, so…

SALLY. Wait outside, Scott, would you?

He skips outside to wait for her. She shuts the door.

Beat.

'Titting shitbag' is kind.

MICHAEL. I called him much much worse. I do recall.

SALLY. He's not a serious contender, is he? My instinct is never to let him back in through the door. (*Pause.*) Sir?

MICHAEL. Was he right? About the mic thing?

SALLY. I thought you didn't care.

MICHAEL. He's perfect. Offer it to him.

SALLY. Oh no, please – come on.

MICHAEL. Talented. Unafraid. AND WE BOTH HATE HIM. Get him back in. He starts tomorrow. Seven a.m.

Scene fades…

Scene Six

Darkness.

Street lights shine at the windows.

A party is in progress in the big dining room downstairs. We can hear the soft music of a small café orchestra and the hum of lively gossip.

ANDREA *enters, wearing a cocktail dress and carrying a glass of champagne. She has a small gaggle of friends with her –* GUESTS *at the party. Giving them the guided tour.*

MICHAEL *tags along, glass in his hand. He's a little softened by the wine.*

ANDREA. Nerve centre.

Turns a light on. The place is a mess – paperwork everywhere.

GUEST 1. Not very glamorous.

MICHAEL (*points*). Drips. Yellow drips. On the paint.

GUEST 2. Drips?

MICHAEL. Nicotine. Cigars.

ANDREA. Three hundred years. Smoke-filled rooms. No one's ever thought to run round with a J-cloth.

One of the assembled company is HEATHER *– still wearing her work suit.*

HEATHER. Is it awful? Are you hating it?

MICHAEL. She's loving it.

ANDREA. Like dressing up and playing in a big old Wendy house.

MICHAEL. Men with machine guns lift her shopping.

ANDREA. Does have a certain flavour of Alice in Wonderland.

A little laughter.

GUEST 1. And… kids settling all right?

MICHAEL (*shrugs*). All right.

ANDREA. I put in extra beds. So they could have friends to stay.

GUEST 2. That's got to be a pretty cool sleepover.

ANDREA. No one's come, of course.

MICHAEL. You have to have background checks.

ANDREA. It must be odd for them. (*Stage whisper.*) Ellie is repeating her GCSE year. Want to make things as normal as possible.

MICHAEL. Yesterday we had a dinner for the bloke who plays Gandalf.

ANDREA. She's a sweetie, my lass.

MICHAEL. She is. She is.

ANDREA. But she does get in an awful state about things.

GUEST 1. You still have tears?

MICHAEL. The move was a wrench.

ANDREA. We've given her the best room. Put her posters up. Changed things round a bit.

Beat.

HEATHER. Can't you get someone in? You know – to decorate.

ANDREA. Frowned on.

HEATHER. By whom?

ANDREA. Oh. The people who frown around here.

HEATHER. We're all so peculiar in this country. Have to make sure our public servants live in penury.

ANDREA. You know the silliest part?

MICHAEL. She's going to say 'holidays'. (*Blows her a kiss.*)

ANDREA. It's summer holidays. Touchpaper. We've been told we're never to go abroad. Cottage in Dorset. Have to go round buying local cheeses.

GUEST 2. What's happening with Chiswick?

MICHAEL. On the market.

GUEST 2. No! You've only just finished doing it up.

ANDREA. Can't afford it.

GUEST 2. Andy, that's criminal.

ANDREA. Michael earns less than the kid's headmaster.

MICHAEL (*shrugs*). Costs these days to be a British Prime Minister. You have to wear a hair shirt and rub gravel on your face. Start planning a new kitchen – they think you're Salome.

HEATHER. What will happen when… you know… you have to leave?

ANDREA. I'm looking round for something. So the kids don't end up in the workhouse.

MICHAEL. Financial minefield.

HEATHER. I had no idea.

ANDREA. I have grumbled a bit but – apparently it's not seemly.

MICHAEL. It's not seemly.

ANDREA *smiles softly at him, links his arm.*

ANDREA. Don't get me wrong – it's lovely and everything. All the parties we'll be hosting. Plus there's Chequers to explore. But… it's not geared up for families. Macmillan was a country squire. We're working parents. (*Headed for the door.*) Come and look at the dishes here. The porcelain.

And she drifts out with her entourage.

HEATHER *hangs back for a moment to speak to* MICHAEL.

We can still hear ANDREA *talking in the next room – see the party hovering just outside the door.*

HEATHER. Must be weird. (*Beat.*) Must be weird. All this.

MICHAEL (*cautious*). There's pudding downstairs. We really ought to go before it's swiped.

HEATHER. We don't know each other that well.

She offers her hand. He takes it reluctantly.

MICHAEL. No.

He lets go. Beat.

HEATHER. Am I making you tense?

MICHAEL. No. This is my personality. Why?

She laughs gently.

HEATHER. This thing – tonight – it's a lovely do.

MICHAEL. They've made little cheesecakes with summer fruits on. Apricots.

HEATHER. I've been hoping. For a chance to meet, I mean. (*Breath.*) Hoping that… gossip isn't all we get to talk about.

He smiles politely and turns to go.

And so she seizes her moment.

How far do you think you're going to get?

MICHAEL. Excuse me?

HEATHER. Freezing out the press.

MICHAEL. I thought you meant 'walking through the door'.

HEATHER. Sorry to be blunt.

MICHAEL. Mm.

HEATHER. Access to you is… limited. I thought I'd seize my moment. Little ambush. Corner you.

He is staring at her with a very odd face – struggling to remember her name.

And then she realises he can't remember.

Heather.

MICHAEL. Yes. Of course. Heather. Took me a moment.

HEATHER. Last time you saw me I was in my pyjamas.

This throws him totally.

Charity party. Chequers. Your wife was hosting.

MICHAEL. Right. All coming back to me. You're the… (*And as he realises his manner changes.*) ah, the columnist.

Beat.

HEATHER. See – that's odd. You can't place me. I write the political column for biggest red top in the country. But you don't know me.

MICHAEL. Pyjama thing threw me.

HEATHER. You don't know my face. Or my name. That's… genuinely surprising.

MICHAEL *turns to leave again.*

Your predecessor – apparently he went around with five hundred mobile-phone numbers in his pocket. All the top people in the land – opinion-makers. Every spare moment he'd call one.

MICHAEL (*his mood turning darker*). 'Opinion-makers'?

HEATHER. Scientists; researchers; the Director of the Opera House. Knew them all by name.

MICHAEL (*a wry smile*). And you're one of those. 'Opinion-makers.'

HEATHER. Can I ask…?

MICHAEL. What entitles you to private chats? I'm fascinated.

Pause.

HEATHER. Well, as I told you…

MICHAEL. You're a journalist. Bravo. Why does that entitle you to a slice of my time?

Beat.

HEATHER. Well, obviously…

MICHAEL. Your job isn't to steer me. It's to wait and see what I do – then toddle off and write your headline.

HEATHER. Well, actually…

MICHAEL (*affable, not aggressive*). Scientists and researchers I get. 'How close are we to curing cancer?' Helps to know. But you don't *lead*. You don't *shape*. You're on the sidelines. What's the vital information I don't have that you could offer?

Oh my God. He is serious.

HEATHER. I could tell you what our readers are thinking.

MICHAEL (*unimpressed*). You talk to them all personally, I suppose.

HEATHER. No, but…

MICHAEL. You could say what your proprietor is thinking. And I could tell you I don't care. So we're done, then. Cheesecake to follow.

He is leaving. She ducks ahead of him and stands in front of the door to keep him in there a while longer.

HEATHER. You've got a problem.

MICHAEL. Yes. I'm missing my pudding.

HEATHER. No – I'm saying you've got a problem with this office.

Beat. He's waiting to hear.

Ten years in Government. Successful ones.

MICHAEL. Yes. Terrible.

HEATHER. Everyone's bored. That's what I'm saying to you.

MICHAEL. Oh, well then…

HEATHER. Depleted stock of headlines. Same old rhetoric. The press love novelty most. You need to give us something new. Decide where you want us to put the focus.

Beat.

MICHAEL. You want me to… *entertain*? Learn some card tricks?

HEATHER. Handle the press or they're going to handle you.

He starts to laugh. Can't help himself. Then finally reins it in.

MICHAEL. Then that's the price.

Beat. She stares at him with a gentle smile.

HEATHER. God. Principles.

MICHAEL. Okay. So you recognise them after all?

HEATHER. Mm. Took me a little while though.

A shared smile.

Scene fades…

Scene Seven

Morning.

MICHAEL, SALLY *and a large gaggle of Private and Parliamentary* SECRETARIES *hovering. Also* DENIS, *who has nabbed the best chair. The regular morning meeting. Everyone crammed in the office. Standing room only.*

SCOTT *loiters quietly at the back of the room, surrounded by the coterie of political officials.*

SALLY *has a whiteboard on the desk in front of her – filling in a grid with information.*

They are all reading identical copies of a white paper.

MICHAEL. You all like it?

Beat.

ADVISER 1. 'S what we need.

ADVISER 2. Definitely.

DENIS. Bold. Energetic. Zesty.

MICHAEL. Why education?

DENIS. 'Why'?

MICHAEL (*nods at the whiteboard*). Why's it earn its place in the grid? Hm?

ADVISER 1. Good piece of legislation. Progressive.

SALLY. What's troubling you about it?

Long beat.

MICHAEL. The wall chart.

ADVISER 1. What?

SALLY (*'Oh no, here we go.'*). Okay, look…

MICHAEL. She's going to come in with a wall chart tucked under her arm. Colour-coding. There'll be colour-coding. Little stickers in… star shapes.

DENIS. What's this actually about, Michael?

MICHAEL. She'll have lots of *phrases*. On cards. A big stack of file cards. Laminated, I bet. Politics and stationery, perfectly combined.

SALLY (*'Oh Christ.'*). And… that's what's bugging you about her Bill, is it?

MICHAEL. I have a vision of her now. Sitting up in bed, shuffling Post-it notes around. Picking just the right shade of… lemon.

DENIS (*assuming this is a joke*). We can't ditch a Bill just because of the stationery.

MICHAEL. Why?

A little nervous laughter in the room.

ADVISER 1. Sir…?

MICHAEL. Education. It's a big fat football. Very easy way to score your first goal. If you're aiming for the top spot in politics – the way to make your name is to shake up British classrooms.

ADVISER 2. Prime Minister…

MICHAEL. She's using this as a leg-up. Launching her fabulous ministerial career. Changing the whole system just to make a splash.

DENIS. Whatever her motives… there are some very good things here.

MICHAEL. You know the ministers I trust? They come in and they plead. HERE'S A BURNING ISSUE. HELP ME!! More money for dementia care. More foreign aid. (*Slaps the Education Bill.*) This isn't an issue. It's just… tinkering.

SALLY. Sir…

MICHAEL. Tinkering! Just to make her mark. Poor old teachers are too damned tired to complain. Walking wounded, all of them. We really want to shake the system up again? (*Throws the paper down.*) Committee.

ADVISER 2. Sir?

MICHAEL. Throw it into committee. Kick it round a bit.

DENIS. Committee's a delaying tactic.

MICHAEL. You bet.

SALLY. Keep-her-sweet-whilst-never-actually-doing-much.

MICHAEL. Put it in committee. It doesn't earn its place on the grid.

SALLY *obliges, scribbling 'Education' at the bottom edge of the grid. Not a priority.* MICHAEL *is passionate and no one chooses to argue.*

Everyone puts away the white paper – takes out a second one. A slimmer volume.

SALLY. Okay. Local Authorities Bill.

MICHAEL (*studies the text eagerly*). Now this I like.

ADVISER 2. Reforming the law on social housing.

DENIS. Splendid.

SCOTT. Minefield.

Everyone looks round.

MICHAEL. Sorry, Scott?

SCOTT. Don't do it. Minefield.

MICHAEL. Housing is everything. Housing is the silver bullet. Can't get a job without a house. Can't have security. Can't have self-esteem. Give a man a house you're giving him… civilisation. You're giving him a place in society.

SCOTT. Nice speech. But not the point.

MICHAEL. Then let's arrive at the point.

SCOTT (*'Isn't it obvious?'*). Sorry. Shall I say? (*To* MICHAEL.) Your wife.

MICHAEL. I beg your pardon?

SCOTT. She's been in the press. On this subject. Complaining.

A cold silence.

MICHAEL. She's been talking… about the Housing Bill?

SCOTT. No. She's been grumbling about living in Number 10. Begging the Treasury for funding. Wants to put in new bedrooms. For your kids.

MICHAEL. We won't discuss that in this meeting. Do you mind?

SCOTT (*nods at the whiteboard*). We're doing 'the grid', yes? This is the weekly *grid meeting*? All the issues we're putting front and centre. Weeding out what could cause us headaches. Well – this is a whopper.

MICHAEL. You want to ditch the Bill… because of my wife?

SCOTT. Sir, if we lead off with this… if this is our flagship legislation… the whole conversation will be 'housing'. We'll be drawing attention to the people who can't get on the ladder. Do we really want to start that conversation with your wife's comments echoing in our ears? Number 10 just ISN'T QUITE GOOD ENOUGH!?

MICHAEL. I don't want my wife's name spoken in this meeting.

A charged pause. DENIS *tries to manage the moment.*

DENIS. We don't pick apart legislation on the off-chance that they might be mean to someone we like.

MICHAEL. The press have rules. Professional conduct.

SCOTT. Any fucker with a laptop and a phone is a journalist!

MICHAEL. What?

SCOTT. Some sly bastard can be mean on the web. Say something bitchy. Won't even have to sign their name.

SALLY. Scott…

SCOTT. And then the national papers can pick it up: 'Look at this shameful thing someone said about your missus.' Comment. It's how they'll use the story. 'Goodlad's wife is whining about her kitchen.' Get it off the grid. She'll be crucified.

And MICHAEL *finally erupts.*

MICHAEL (*slams his fist into the desk – papers fly*). I DON'T WANT YOU TALKING ABOUT HER IN HERE. YOU UNDERSTAND ME??

Silence.

I want to do something for my country. My conceited notion I can… serve the people in some way. My wife – she's a civilian.

SCOTT. No.

MICHAEL. What??

SCOTT. She's not. Because you are giving nothing away!! No interviews, no Sunday-morning radio, no profile pieces. You've starved them and they're ravenous. Mrs Goodlad is the next best thing.

MICHAEL. I'm sorry. I won't ditch it. It's… it's crossing a line.

SCOTT. Yes. Okay. But…

MICHAEL. This is work that needs doing. Houses that need building. People that need getting off the street. If someone wants to say something shitty about my wife…

SCOTT. Sir…

MICHAEL. …we don't hobble the Government because of it!!

Silence.

SALLY. Okay.

Still a silence.

Okay. We should move on.

Just the sound of turning pages. And then…

SCOTT. Sorry. Not yet. No. I'm paid to do a job here and I'm doing it.

SALLY. Scott…

SCOTT. Sack me for being irritating, yes. But you're never going to sack me for failing in this office.

SALLY. Scott…

SCOTT. She will become the story. Putting the Bill front and centre now is just naive. Launch it next week. Next month. JUST NOT TODAY.

Long beat. MICHAEL *is deciding.*

MICHAEL (*murmurs*). I came here to be fearless.

SCOTT. But you're not. You're afraid for her. Admit it.

Long beat.

MICHAEL *looks at* SALLY.

MICHAEL. Okay.

SALLY. What does 'okay' mean?

MICHAEL. Okay. Yes. It's off the grid. Just for the time being.

SALLY *is astonished at this little victory from* SCOTT. *She shuffles over to* MICHAEL, *speaks quietly so no one can hear.*

SALLY. Did what-I-think-just-happened… actually happen? Did you just allow the bellhop to dictate strategy?

But before MICHAEL *can answer her…*

ADVISER 1. Education Secretary's outside. You said you'd give her your response.

Door opens. In walks PRISCILLA *– Minister for Education. With a big coloured chart rolled up under her arm.*

PRISCILLA. Prime Minister. Thanks for finding the time.

MICHAEL. Not at all. Oh, you've got a wall chart there. Let's see it.

Scene fades…

Scene Eight

Late in the evening.

A big mess of papers left over from the day's events.

MICHAEL *is alone, sitting, staring at nothing. Drowning in paper.*

A tray in front of him with the remnants of some sandwiches.

Knock at the door. STEWARD *arrives, sees him there.*

STEWARD. Oh, sorry, sir.

MICHAEL. No, it's fine.

STEWARD. May I just tidy up?

And the STEWARD *starts to deposit rubbish into the bin.*

ANDREA *enters.*

ANDREA. Any chance we're going to see you this evening? Ben's got his heart set on doing a jigsaw.

MICHAEL. I was just thinking about…

ANDREA. What?

MICHAEL. …coming here. My decision.

She sits with him.

I remember watching *News24*. Watching my colleagues throw their hats into the ring. (*Breathes deep, speaks wistfully.*) Watching them parade on camera, obeying the rules, doing the little dance. 'Don't wear stripes on TV or it will dazzle.' 'Don't stare at one journalist for more than eight seconds.' They send us on courses to learn this stuff. 'If you don't like the question then don't repeat it.' I watched their wives kiss them on cue and give their best smiles. And I thought 'They've done the same course I have.' (*Pause. Sighs.*) As if the only route to success – the only route was this… square dance in front of the media. I watched – and I knew I had to stand.

ANDREA. What's happened? Something's happened.

MICHAEL. I thought I was immune. Turns out… I'm not.

ANDREA. 'Immune'? (*Beat.*) What's going on?

MICHAEL. You probably shouldn't complain about our lives in a room where there are journalists.

ANDREA. Oh. I see. It's something *I've* done. (*Stands to leave.*) If we're going to have a row, can we postpone? I have an appointment with a jigsaw.

And she's gone.

The STEWARD *smiles politely at him.*

MICHAEL. Sorry, sorry. I'll get out of your way.

The salad on his tray is untouched.

I never eat the garnish.

STEWARD. I must get to know you better, sir.

He takes the garnish off and puts it on the tray. The STEWARD *whisks it away.*

Scene fades…

Scene Nine

Mid-afternoon.

MICHAEL *and* SALLY.

MICHAEL *is pacing, angry, agitated.*

MICHAEL. She's been summoned?

SALLY. I made it quite clear. 'Drop whatever you're doing and get over.'

MICHAEL. Scott, as well. We need Scott in the room.

SALLY. He's on his way. Let's just all be calm and consider…

Door flies open. PRISCILLA *enters.*

PRISCILLA. Prime Minister.

MICHAEL. What are you doing to us?

PRISCILLA. Okay, look…

MICHAEL. We speak with one voice. Or we're totally out of control.

PRISCILLA. It happened fast. There was an ambush.

MICHAEL. You did the rope line. That's not an ambush! That's a sodding interview!!

Door flies open. It's SCOTT. *He is desperate to find out what occurred.*

SCOTT. What happened?

SALLY. It's okay, we're sorting it.

PRISCILLA. I got a question on the rope line. On the street. Just this morning. (*Deep breath.*) There was a badly arranged rope line.

SCOTT. Oh yes, fine. Let's blame the cops on duty.

PRISCILLA. Someone called out a question.

MICHAEL. And you took it.

PRISCILLA. I took it.

MICHAEL. About?

SCOTT (*'Isn't it obvious?'*). Her Education Bill.

Beat.

PRISCILLA. Why was it stuck in committee?

SALLY. You told them – what?

PRISCILLA. I said… I may have hinted…

SCOTT. Oh fuck.

PRISCILLA. I said it was… (*Treading lightly.*) delayed at your request.

They all stare at her.

SCOTT. 'Delayed'?

PRISCILLA (*rallying*). Well, it *was* wasn't it? Put into committee.

MICHAEL. 'Delayed.'

SCOTT. You've handed them their headline. You've handed them a potential… rift.

PRISCILLA. Now, look…

SCOTT (*to* PRISCILLA). You're trying to push ahead with reforms. And we're the bad guys. You – you're the great crusader, trying to raise standards. We're just in your way. You could have said 'consultation period'? You could have just walked past? Instead you had to piss all over us!

Everyone shocked by SCOTT*'s choice of phrase. They look to* MICHAEL *to respond but he says nothing.*

PRISCILLA. Do you want me to issue a statement?

SCOTT. Can I draft it for you?

PRISCILLA. I have my people, thank you.

SCOTT. Not doing a very good job, are they? Letting you loose out there. Dropping shit-bombs.

PRISCILLA. I beg your pardon??

And SCOTT *finally loses his temper.*

SCOTT. Fucking amateurs.

SALLY. Scotty.

SCOTT. Fucking children. They should leave governing to the grown-ups.

PRISCILLA (*to* MICHAEL). I'm a minister. I won't be spoken to this way. (*Nodding at* SCOTT.) Who the hell is this? What's he doing here?

MICHAEL. Could you please leave us?

And she leaves.

Silence once she has gone.

SCOTT *takes out his laptop and starts to surf.*

SALLY. She's got a point.

Beat. No response from anyone.

Sorry, but she has. If anyone's going to admonish her it should be you, sir. Scott's not entitled to wade in…

MICHAEL. Let's not do this now, okay? Let's just fix the problem.

SCOTT. You were right about her career trajectory. Woman is DESPERATE FOR YOUR JOB. She gets the glory and you get the shit – all in one enormous sexy dollop. You see the way she came in here with her little apology all rehearsed. There'll be a story about her struggle to drag education forwards. And how you kiboshed her. (*Breathes deep.*) I told you – a void gets filled. This is going to run and run and run. We've given them five weeks of policy policy policy. Dull as fucking dishwater. This is the juice they wanted.

SALLY. Why was it sent to committee? Why was it taken off the grid? We need an answer.

SCOTT. There's already speculation.

SALLY. What?

SCOTT. Look. Already online. 'Goodlad drags his feet on school reform.' (*Beat as he reads the opening paragraph.*) It mentions Ellie.

MICHAEL. What???

SCOTT. Mentions your daughter.

MICHAEL. Why???

SCOTT. Still at school. Repeating her final year. Reckons that's why you've put the brake on. Waiting until your daughter's gone through the system.

MICHAEL. IT SAYS THAT??

SCOTT. 'Goodlad is protecting his own brood from all the sweeping reforms that are planned. His own daughter is repeating a year at her state school owing to tragic personal circumstances.'

He grabs the laptop from SCOTT *and reads it.*

Long pause.

And then he smashes the laptop on the desk. Volcanically angry.

Everyone is silent.

MICHAEL. She suffered some problems.

SALLY. You don't have to say…

SCOTT (*holds up hand to silence her*). Hold on. He does. I need to understand.

MICHAEL. She took some pills. Doctors said she was depressed. We got a call from school to say she hadn't come in one morning. Andy… she came home and found her. Rushed her into hospital. It was… (*But he can't finish.*)

SALLY. We're not talking about it.

SCOTT. No. But *they are*. Internet forums. I warned you. No regulation. They can say what they fucking like. Then tomorrow the papers will pick it up. They'll have had the story sitting in a drawer for a while. No reason to run it. But

– today it's open season. 'Twitter storm rages about the PM's daughter.' That's a headline.

Beat.

MICHAEL (*head in hand*). She had all sorts of issues. She had problems with bullying for a while. God, it makes me sick. To think *her* name is out there. Talked about. TALKED ABOUT. By… people. A public commodity.

SCOTT (*forcing him to focus*). There are things I can do. To keep the press from getting on her case. Give them a belter.

SALLY *looks at him, concerned.*

It's the way the game is played. A story big enough to obliterate this. To buy their silence.

Beat. MICHAEL *not responding.*

Leaked minutes. (*Beat.*) Think of the most explosive meeting you've had in weeks. Leak the minutes. Right now. Today. We can point the finger of suspicion at some hapless bloody intern.

Still silence in the room. No one sure what to do. SCOTT *presses the point.*

We leak the most damaging set of minutes we can lay our hands on. Ellie slips off the radar.

A long pause whilst MICHAEL *decides.*

MICHAEL. Don't tell me what. Just –

Beat.

SCOTT. What? (*Beat.*) What? (*Beat.*) Say it. (*Beat.*) Am I off the leash?

Blackout.

ACT TWO

Scene Ten

Some weeks later. MICHAEL *is preparing for Prime Minister's Questions – reading extracts from his speech, written out on file cards.*

SCOTT *loiters, heckling him in the most mild-mannered way imaginable.*

The room has a much more lived-in look – plenty of mess, papers scattered around. And SCOTT *has acquired his own 'area' – a corner table stacked with folders.*

MICHAEL. 'Some of you will recall a time…'

SCOTT (*mutters*). Bollocks.

MICHAEL. '…when hospital trusts were first introduced in this country.'

SCOTT. Bollocks. Bollocks.

MICHAEL. 'The accusation was that…'

SCOTT. Bollocks.

MICHAEL. '…there would be…'

SCOTT. Arse.

MICHAEL. '…a two-tier system.'

SCOTT. Total shit-wank. What a load of shit-wank!

MICHAEL *looks up from his card.*

Problem?

MICHAEL. They're never going to say 'shit-wank'.

SCOTT. Granted. No.

MICHAEL. They say 'shame' a lot.

SCOTT. I was going for tone not content.

MICHAEL. You really think that this is necessary?

SCOTT. Well I'm enjoying it.

MICHAEL. Right-oh. (*Back to the notes.*) 'The reality has been quite the opposite.'

SCOTT. Cock. The man is talking cock. Sack him. Boo!

MICHAEL. 'In fact… trusts have attracted true professionals. People who really want to make a difference.'

Knock on the door.

SALLY *enters with* DENIS.

SCOTT. What a lot of shit! Big lumpy shit! This man deserves a kicking.

SALLY. The Chairman.

DENIS. Did I come at the wrong time?

MICHAEL. Conditioning.

DENIS. What?

SCOTT. Man's an arsehole. And he's fat. (*To* DENIS.) Join in, why don't ya? It's cool to swear.

MICHAEL. Firing blanks. Scott has insisted we do this before Prime Minister's Questions. All part of his… 'regime'. Trying to 'toughen me up' apparently.

DENIS. Ah. Okay. Sorry. Yes.

MICHAEL. Just… let me get to the end. (*Finishes.*) 'Hospital trusts have revolutionised…'

SCOTT. Toss.

MICHAEL. '…the health…'

SCOTT. Toss.

MICHAEL. '…system.'

SCOTT. Come on, Mr Chairman, you're not trying. We give him a hard time in here so that down the road later it will seem like a sleigh ride.

DENIS. Right. You want me to…?

MICHAEL. 'They've raised the standard.'

SCOTT. Lame-arse!

MICHAEL. 'Now healthcare is improving at a faster rate…

SCOTT. Total piss.

MICHAEL. '…in every region.'

SCOTT (*to* DENIS). Get in his face.

DENIS. Yes?

MICHAEL. 'A&E waiting times are falling…'

SCOTT (*to* DENIS). Go on.

MICHAEL. '…year on year.'

SCOTT. Lay into him.

DENIS (*with surprising vigour*). BALL-BAGS!!

Beat.

MICHAEL. I'd finished.

Beat.

DENIS. Sorry. Thought I was helping.

MICHAEL *folds his speech away.*

You asked to see me.

SCOTT. *I* did.

DENIS. Sorry?

MICHAEL. Scott did.

DENIS. Oh. Okay. *Scott*.

SCOTT. Honours list.

DENIS. Yes.

SCOTT. The consultations. We came to you for advice. Who to honour.

DENIS. Yes. You did.

SCOTT. 'Who deserves OBEs?' 'Who gets gold braid?'

DENIS. I gave my recommendations.

They steer DENIS *to a chair.*

SCOTT. So… you have some idea who's getting one. You're on the inside.

DENIS. Yes. Is this a press issue?

MICHAEL. We need to rap your knuckles. Just a bit.

SCOTT. The press have got hold of some names.

MICHAEL. It's not a tragedy, of course.

SCOTT. But it's a leak. Hence – you're here. Hence – this meeting.

Beat. DENIS *looks from* MICHAEL *to* SCOTT *and back again.*

DENIS. Leak?

SCOTT. Yes.

Beat.

DENIS. It didn't come from me.

SCOTT. You sure? You talked to Simon Wilson of the *Guardian*.

DENIS (*laughing*). Do you have spies?

SCOTT (*dead-pan*). Everywhere. EVERYWHERE. I know what you had from the dessert trolley. I know if you had custard or cream with it.

DENIS. Look…

SCOTT. What were the *terms* of your conversation?

DENIS. 'Terms'?

SCOTT. Oh dear. And you don't even know the word.

DENIS. Scott…

SCOTT. 'On the record', 'off the record', 'deep background', 'unnamed source', 'no fingerprints'?

DENIS. Er… he's… doing a piece. I'm a coin collector. Someone's taking a photo at our home.

SCOTT. Spiffing. And?

DENIS. We spoke.

SCOTT. About coin collecting? Anything else?

DENIS. Why am I being interrogated?

SCOTT *sits next to him, sighs like a disappointed parent.*

SCOTT. You made a mistake. A basic blunder. Not defining *terms*. You mentioned the honours list.

DENIS. Possibly.

SCOTT. 'Possibly'? He passed it on to his news desk.

DENIS. I… I said I was chuffed. I said one… particular actress was a favourite.

SCOTT. You gave him a name.

DENIS. I wasn't divulging state secrets.

MICHAEL. Honours list is a delicate time. We love having your input, of course. But. We'd prefer to keep the names as… classified.

Beat. DENIS *rather ruffled.*

DENIS. I think you're making rather a lot of this.

MICHAEL. It's important to Scott.

SCOTT. It's important to me.

DENIS (*to* MICHAEL). I apologise.

MICHAEL. Not necessary.

DENIS. Is that the whole meeting?

MICHAEL. Yes. See you at PMQ.

DENIS. Right.

DENIS *slopes out, chastened.*

SCOTT. Jesus. JESUS.

MICHAEL. Where's my file?

And SCOTT *trots out of the opposite door to fetch it.*

Chairman's a bloody old gossip. A liability.

SALLY. And that's just how you made him feel. Not sure what it earned you – bringing him here and humiliating him.

MICHAEL. Scotty's got a job to do.

SALLY. And you're happy for him to talk like that. To Party people?

MICHAEL. Sal…

SALLY. Honours list – there are always rumblings. Why's he so paranoid about keeping this year secret?

MICHAEL *stares at her – what is she implying?*

MICHAEL. Doesn't look good, if it comes out early.

SALLY. 'Doesn't look good'? Uh-huh. That's it? That's all? (*Beat. She's not convinced by his answer. Suggesting her own theory:*) If someone leaks it… he can't leak it himself. He can't sell a story that's already been sold.

Beat. MICHAEL *is not responding.*

Michael?

MICHAEL. You remember what happened with Ellie.

SALLY. Yes. We panicked. We got scared for her. We let him make ONE TACTICAL LEAK. But if he starts making a habit of it we are going to get bloody crucified. We made ourselves holier-than-thou. If he's leaking and he gets found out we are going to pay a heavy price.

MICHAEL. Sal…

SALLY. You've told him to keep the cupboard full. 'Keep some stories handy.' Just in case there's a next time.

MICHAEL. Okay. Yes. It's… ammunition. Just in case. I don't want… petty nonsense to destroy us! I've got too much I want to achieve. It's a political necessity. It won't get out of hand.

SALLY. Write that down. Write down the EXACT DATE AND TIME YOU SAID THAT.

Door opens. SCOTT *comes back in with file, interrupts their conversation.*

SCOTT. Ready? Let's go get 'em.

And they head off to PMQ.

Scene fades…

Scene Eleven

Midday.

Defence briefing.

The lights are extinguished. The curtains are drawn. A video projector shows classified shots of the Middle East conflict: tank formations and missile launches.

The briefing is lead by GENERAL SIR ALASTAIR HUME – *Chief of the Defence Staff.*

Also present is SALLY, SCOTT *and a number of* MILITARY ADVISERS *in uniform. The whole meeting is crisp and formal.*

HUME. Our presence is diminished, of course. Three out of four regions where we had a US mandate – we no longer have a military force. And in the fourth region…

Click. The video image changes.

…withdrawn our troops to the Airbase.

Click.

What remains is a small but active force. A pilot light. Hand-holding for the Americans. Barely five hundred troops on the ground.

MICHAEL. Their significance is not just military.

HUME. Ostensibly political. With us in place it's still an international force. We withdraw – the Americans look like… conquerors. We need to give them self-government. But we need to remain. To support the US effort.

Beat. Click of a switch. Video projector dies.

Lights come on again.

Pause. A little muttering amongst the military staff.

Prime Minister?

MICHAEL. Picked me up in a golf cart. Do you remember that?

HUME. I'm not following you, sir.

MICHAEL. July. The thing at Camp David. He picked me up from the plane in a golf cart. The President.

HUME. Ah.

Beat. No one sure where this is going.

MICHAEL. Four weeks. Four weeks of back-and-forth about that summit. Who should be wearing what? We insisted on suits, of course. They wanted open-necked shirts and jeans. More casual.

HUME. Yes, sir…

MICHAEL. We were so damned careful. We wanted to look professional, not like pals. Not like… cowboys on the range. And then the golf cart. Made me look a twat.

SALLY. Sir…

HUME. You're upset about the arrangements.

No reply.

But if we can put that to one side…?

MICHAEL. You want me to commit us to three more years, just to help the US with their image? That's your advice. (*Beat.*) That's not going to happen.

HUME. Sir…

MICHAEL. Making them 'seem' they're not conquerors. MAKING THEM SEEM. You're asking me to put people's lives at risk to make… John Wayne look good on screen.

HUME. Sir…

MICHAEL. There's no strategic necessity. No reason at all for us to be there.

HUME. I believe…

MICHAEL. I want a possible stop date. Give me a possible stop date.

HUME. I'd prefer we don't talk numbers.

MICHAEL. You'd *prefer it*??

HUME. We never brief in hard numbers. Hard numbers are difficult to adhere to, in a war zone.

MICHAEL. You're saying if you pick a date to leave… we might have to shift it around, if they start firing at you.

HUME (*masking his irritation*). Yes, indeed.

MICHAEL. Well, I appreciate the problem. You don't want to set a target you can't meet. But – here's my problem. I've got all these young men here and some of them are dying so the US can keep up their image.

Silence.

I want a number. I want a date. Don't ever come to me with this again. I know you're trained to use a gun but it doesn't actually intimidate me. Now get on with it.

SCOTT *can't resist a smile*. GENERAL HUME *nods curtly.*

Scene fades…

Scene Twelve

Senior staff meeting.

MICHAEL, SALLY, SCOTT, *and huge numbers of political* ADVISERS *and* SECRETARIES.

SALLY *is running the meeting.* MICHAEL *is sitting with his feet up, wading through some documents. Not fully engaged.*

SALLY. Okay. Let's run through it from the top.

ADVISER 1 (*glancing at a memo*). This week at a glance.

ADVISER 2. Go, us. We're on a roll.

SALLY (*from the list*). Four hundred thousand in donations.

ADVISER 1. And he's a prominent business name. Good to have him in our stable.

SALLY. What next?

ADVISER 3. Just two votes to find on the Bill.

SALLY. Whoa. Two votes away from the promised land. (*To* MICHAEL.) You going to see some wobblers? Take their temperature?

MICHAEL. Let the Whips have a crack at them first. What else?

SALLY. General Hume has – rather grudgingly – set out a departure strategy for the troops.

Some congratulatory applause.

(*Anticipating* MICHAEL*'s question.*) Yes, there is a date. November 15th, it starts.

ADVISER 1. Week after Remembrance Sunday. Very poetic.

SALLY. You'll be the man who got the troops back home by Christmas. That's something to celebrate. And to cap it all – here's our report card. (*Digs out a document.*) God bless Ipsos MORI. Sixty-one-per-cent approval.

General excitement at this.

Yep. Hang on. Let's not start group-hugging just yet. There's still the book to discuss. The 'kiss and tell'. (*Beat.*) Anyone read it?

No nods. No hands go up.

Anyone getting it for Christmas? (*Beat.*) I need some input here. A key member of this Party – an ex-minister, gone on record. Every ghastly little recollection. Where are we with this? It's not very flattering about this office.

Beat. She looks around for input.

ADVISER 1. He's entitled to write a book.

SALLY. This isn't a meeting on the ethics of publishing. The thing is being serialised. Could mean trouble. Next four weeks in the *Observer*. Strategy? Anyone?

No responses.

No?

ADVISER 2 (*shrugs*). He's a spent force. Everyone knows it.

Murmurs of agreement.

SALLY. Everyone will still buy the paper though, right? We need to know where the blows are going to come.

SCOTT (*to* MICHAEL). He says you once told him to 'fuck off and resign'.

Some laughter.

Here. In this office.

SALLY. You've read it?

SCOTT. Of course I've read it. I got galleys a week ago.

SALLY. When I asked if anyone had read it you didn't put your hand up.

SCOTT (*ice-cold*). I forgot that we were in a classroom.

MICHAEL. I never told him to 'fuck off'.

ADVISER 1. Okay. So we can challenge the facts. That's a reasonable start.

MICHAEL. I told him to 'bugger off', I think.

SCOTT (*dry*). Well, that distinction's going to be pretty valuable.

More laughter.

MICHAEL. I told him if he didn't resign… I would sack him. I told him I couldn't tolerate him at all. He started on about… how he was one of my best people. Day of the reshuffle.

SALLY. Well, his book takes the view that you sacked the most successful chancellor in a decade… just because of personal differences.

MICHAEL. Sounds like a page-turner. Must get hold of a copy.

SALLY. Scott?

SCOTT (*hunts for a copy of the galleys in his notes*). *Clive Weatherley: Memoirs*. A lament from someone who's ended on the dung pile. He says everything we fear he might say. Michael's a bruiser with no ability to reach the electorate. Rambles on about lack of focus, inability to transmit beyond that door.

MICHAEL. Does he say anything nice at all?

SCOTT. We serve a good cup of coffee.

MICHAEL. Oh, well there we are.

Shared laughter.

ADVISER 2. We need a strategy. To deal with it.

SCOTT. I'll deal with it.

MICHAEL. Okay. I've got a thing now. Are we done?

MICHAEL *just starting to shuffle papers away, the meeting breaking up gradually.*

SALLY. How?

SCOTT. What?

SALLY. How are you dealing with it?

SCOTT. Steal his lunch money. Trip him over in the playground.

SALLY. Scott…

SCOTT. You don't really need to know, do you? I mean, you don't want an exact game plan.

SALLY. You're going to challenge him to a fist fight? Tickle him? Touch him up?

MICHAEL. Sal…

SALLY. I'd prefer to know what is being done.

Beat.

SCOTT. There are ways.

SALLY. Oh, well, that sounds lovely.

SCOTT. Look, my office is just next door. Let's reconvene….

SALLY. Yes. God forbid that Michael should hear. Let's just wrap him up in cotton wool.

She looks at MICHAEL*, yearning for him to comment. But he doesn't.*

I need to know.

SCOTT. I will empty my pockets. I will sprinkle lollipops up and down the length of Fleet Street. They don't want to crucify us AS MUCH AS THEY WANT TO SELL THEIR HORRIBLE SHIT.

SALLY. You're going to sell them something? A leak? A smear? A nasty personal story about him? (*To* MICHAEL.) Sixty-one-per-cent approval rating. This is stupidity. We don't need to do this.

SCOTT. Hang on…

SALLY. We don't need to start leaking to the press at the first sign of trouble, just because we can. WE WERE GOING TO BE BETTER THAN THIS.

And SCOTT *sneers at this.*

Don't fucking smile at me. (*Beat.*) Where will we draw the line once we start?

Still staring hard at MICHAEL*. And finally…*

MICHAEL. You know what it could do to us – slow death – weekly serialisation.

SALLY. So… you're telling him to go ahead.

MICHAEL. Not at all. I'm… open to other strategies.

But she doesn't have any.

I'm eager to hear one.

Scene fades…

Scene Thirteen

The annual party for the Number 10 domestic staff.

People circulate with canapés and sherry. The office is packed. Bubbly chatter.

MICHAEL *is with the* CURATOR FROM CHEQUERS – *a rather starchy woman in a tweed suit.*

SCOTT *lurks near to them in the mêlée, surfing his phone. He has clearly been drinking.*

CURATOR. It's a shame. Terrible shame.

MICHAEL. Mm-hm.

CURATOR. Prime Ministers have always found it such an asset. A second home. With history. Perpendicular Gothic.

MICHAEL. Not my bag to be honest.

CURATOR. Some of the antiquities are breathtaking. Chamberlain's diaries? Did you see them?

SCOTT (*snorts, murmurs*). Woo-hoo.

CURATOR. Churchill turned the upstairs gallery into a cinema. You could have some fun there too.

MICHAEL. The issue is the routine.

CURATOR. I'm sorry?

MICHAEL. We didn't find it to be all that… flexible. If you're not hungry at five o'clock it's tough. You eat when the staff dictate. And we've got children.

CURATOR. Yes, of course, but…

MICHAEL. I caused a riot when we last came. I asked for a satsuma. The fruit bowl had been locked up for the night.

CURATOR. There is the morale. Of my staff.

MICHAEL. You want to feel useful.

SCOTT. Mwah. Shouldn't have swiped the fruit bowl should you, love?

She looks sharply at him.

CURATOR. Prime Minister…

MICHAEL. That thing with my son. He's five.

CURATOR. Mm. We have some very precious items.

MICHAEL. He broke a clock. I have things that are precious too. My family and Chequers – they don't mix.

SCOTT. He's not coming. End of.

She summons her composure, smiles politely and disappears into the mêlée. And SCOTT *laughs cruelly.*

SALLY *swans over, having overheard.*

SALLY. Well, that was lovely.

SCOTT. Starchy cow.

MICHAEL (*murmurs*). Pity, really. Don't want to offend her but – there we are.

And MICHAEL *disappears into the mêlée too.*

SCOTT. She's learned her lesson.

SALLY. I dare say. That was exactly like watching a street gang.

SCOTT *just shrugs, drinks some more.*

Woman has devoted her life to that place.

SCOTT. How many rooms do you think she's wanked off in?

SALLY *very offended, pulls the face.*

Oops. 'Scuse me. Got the stare.

Beat. SALLY *stares at him contemptuously. And then* SCOTT *drifts away.*

SALLY. He shouldn't be here.

MICHAEL. This party?

SALLY. This party, this office. Shouldn't be in Number 10 even.

Beat. MICHAEL *just stares at her.*

I'm serious.

MICHAEL. No, you're not. YOU'RE NOT.

SALLY. Michael, listen…

MICHAEL (*looking around at the other* GUESTS). Please, let's not do this now.

SALLY. Place totally intoxicates him. Walks around like his cock is dragging on the carpet.

Beat. Nothing from MICHAEL.

What's the attraction, Michael? You should have great people working around you – great minds. Instead you've given the office next door to a pit bull.

MICHAEL (*a low angry mutter*). I put myself in a shooting gallery – soon as I took office. He's the only one able to defend me.

SALLY. Sir…

MICHAEL. He gives me cover. He *allows me to be me*. I need to drag this country forwards – Scott clears the path for me.

SALLY. He's not clearing your path, he's sprinkling it with turds.

MICHAEL. He rescued Ellie.

SALLY. Ah. That. *Again*.

MICHAEL (*a rising tide of sound*). Listen, whilst you all stood by… whilst you wrung your hands and gave me a sad little smile. Scott went into the trenches. SAVED MY FAMILY. I need him. He can protect us. That's the punchline.

They are speaking far too loud. Now everyone is listening.

SALLY. I get it. *I get it*. Your own personal attack dog at your side. I can see the appeal of having your own little assassin, spraying bullets. But you're addicted.

MICHAEL. What?

SALLY. To having him around. You're the most decent man I know and yet you keep some… yob in your shadow. You don't know the damage, Michael.

MICHAEL. 'Damage'?

SALLY. To you. To the idea of you. To everything. The brand Michael Goodlad. You see the gossip on the internet last week? The thing about Weatherley, just before his book came out?

MICHAEL. I don't read gossip.

SALLY. Of course! You turn a blind eye! And that makes you clean. That makes you minty-fresh. Doesn't matter that the dog who does it is right next door.

MICHAEL. Did he sign his name?

SALLY. Oh, don't be so bloody naive. He ripped Weatherley apart. HIM! Character assassination. Blow after blow. It had his bloody fingerprints all over it. You can't pretend it didn't happen JUST BECAUSE YOU NEVER GAVE THE ORDER!! Get rid of him!

MICHAEL. I can't. I CAN'T.

SALLY. Michael…

MICHAEL. You think I get to be me in a place like this without some sort of protection? Mouthing off to the Defence Chief of Staff. Telling him I want to drag our troops back home again. Fixing a date!! You think I get to be the great social reformer without making enemies? POWERFUL PEOPLE HATE ME. I need someone who's willing to be brutal – because that's just how my attackers come at me.

ANDREA *scuttles over and tries to quieten them down.*

ANDREA. All okay?

SALLY (*talking to* MICHAEL *about* SCOTT). I can't work with him. I'm done.

ANDREA. What's happening?

MICHAEL. Sally's threatening to resign.

ANDREA. God – no. Sal – why?

MICHAEL. Say it. Go on.

Beat.

SALLY. Scott. It's Scott. I can't work alongside him.

ANDREA (*deflated*). Ah. (*Goes silent. And then…*) He's done… rather a lot for us all. (*Breath.*) We don't want to lose him. (*Breath.*) We don't want to lose you either. But Scott's a fighter.

Scene fades…

Scene Fourteen

MICHAEL *alone in his office. Sits at his desk.*

Straightens his cuff, fidgets until he gets comfortable. Preparations for a meeting.

Long pause whilst he waits.

Then footsteps. And a knock.

SCOTT *opens the door, enters with* HEATHER.

HEATHER. Hi.

MICHAEL. Hi.

HEATHER. Hi. (*Awkward breath.*) Good to see you.

MICHAEL. Thanks. For agreeing to do this… thing today.

He gestures to the seat opposite, and she sits.

HEATHER. How are you?

MICHAEL. Have we started already?

HEATHER. Should have known better than to ask, really, shouldn't I?

She takes out a pad and pen. He views them suspiciously on the desk between them.

SCOTT. Leave you to it.

SCOTT *leaves, and this is the signal for them to begin.*

HEATHER. Okay.

MICHAEL (*trying to smile*). We thought… this was… necessary.

HEATHER (*nodding at the door*). 'We.'

MICHAEL. Face to face. Interview on the record. And… obviously *we* picked *you* because…

HEATHER. Your first one-to-one. I'm honoured. (*Beat.*) There you go. Dispensed with all the nonsense.

An awkward pause. And then they both smile and laugh a little.

And then…

MICHAEL. There's ground we need to cover.

HEATHER. I've been given my list here.

MICHAEL. Health care.

HEATHER. Sure.

MICHAEL. And the problems with Korea.

HEATHER. Can we talk a bit about your staffing crisis? (*Beat.*) Chief of Staff.

MICHAEL. Not on the list. (*Beat.*) That's not on the list.

HEATHER. Well, we're talking about it already – so… let's finish the conversation.

MICHAEL. You're talking about it. *I'm not*. It's a personal issue.

Beat.

HEATHER. A 'personal issue'. (*Likes this phrase – she starts to write it down.*)

MICHAEL (*regrets his choice of words*). Well, a bit…

HEATHER. Chief of Staff resigns. 'Personal' refers to this… feud.

MICHAEL. There hasn't been a feud.

HEATHER. There's been talk of a feud.

MICHAEL. People move on.

Beat. He says nothing. So…

HEATHER. That's what you're saying in response?

Pause.

MICHAEL. Look…

She pointedly puts her pen down and relaxes her posture.

HEATHER. The reason you invited me here – the reason you're doing this, and I know how you hate it – you're getting a bit of bad press since Sally Gaminara walked out. It's taken the sheen off things.

MICHAEL. I'm not responding to it.

HEATHER. You are. *You are*. Or you wouldn't have let me through the door. You're responding by studiously ignoring it. Talk about it. Tackle it and move on.

Beat.

MICHAEL. I'm not giving you that story.

HEATHER. Yes. You are. The fact that you're doing an interview… It says YOU THINK YOU NEED TO DO AN INTERVIEW. To project an image of business as usual.

She leaves a pause, waiting for him to crucify himself.

MICHAEL. I'm not giving you that story. Or anything remotely like it. So. What's next? (*Beat.*) I'll talk policy until the mountains crumble. That's personalities.

HEATHER. And that's a dirty word, isn't it? (*Beat.*) People like personality politics. They trust it, actually. They want to smell your breath. You get all sore about guarding your privacy but… it makes you look evasive… hiding here in your fortress.

Beat. Still nothing from him.

You've got less than eight months till you go to the polls. To most of us you're a stranger. They need to be *sold* a version of you. I'm actually saying this as a friend.

MICHAEL. I beg your pardon?

And she leans in, more intimate than ever.

HEATHER. You need me. Can we be honest about it? At critical moments like this. To carry the message. Well, the message you should carry isn't policy. It's you. The bloke. YOU NEED TO INJECT SOME PERSONALITY.

MICHAEL. Look… (*Swallows his frustration, reins it in.*) You want to ask about health care; you want to ask about taxation policy – fine!

HEATHER. I can get that from a briefing paper. I've come to meet the man.

MICHAEL. I'm sorry, I find this excruciating.

HEATHER. I know. I know. But we live in a world where personality is all. You've had a crisis. Discuss it. Go on. You risk looking out of touch – like you haven't noticed things are going wrong.

MICHAEL. Attlee!

HEATHER. What?

MICHAEL. Made the welfare state – remember him? Stitched this country together with his bare hands. Attlee comes out of Downing Street, on the day of his greatest triumph – someone jams a microphone in his face and points a camera. 'Prime Minister, do you have any message for the country?' Know what Attlee answered??

HEATHER (*seen it*). He said 'no'.

MICHAEL. THE CAMERA WAS AN IRRELEVANCE. Didn't trouble him. Didn't have to make love to it.

HEATHER. Yes, okay, but…

MICHAEL. That door – that bloody step outside – it's not a podium. It's a threshold, for walking in and out. Three feet of concrete for scraping your boots. Suddenly it's become a stage.

HEATHER. Okay. But what's the reason you won't…?

MICHAEL. Bloody Party Conference is no longer about debate – the voice of the rank and file. It's become about lighting states. It's Glastonbury. Without the mud, the drugs and the circus skills. I have been born into an age where a TV interview or a press release has become massively more important than actually doing the fucking job.

HEATHER. Yes! And that's shocking. Totally. But… it *is* the situation so why don't we embrace it? One remark: one comment about your kids. I print it. The people swoon. Another million votes in the bank.

MICHAEL (*and this stops him in his tracks*). A comment. About my kids.

HEATHER. It's like… you're embarrassed to be *who you are*.

MICHAEL. I mention my kids. The people swoon.

HEATHER. Let me help you here. Fatherhood is a vote-winner.

MICHAEL *stands, can't contain himself any longer. It's over.*

MICHAEL. Sorry, but YOU ARE NEITHER AS IMPORTANT NOR AS POWERFUL AS YOU WISH TO BE. Don't pretend like you're a force to be reckoned with. Don't confuse having a voice with having any influence.

SCOTT *hears the furore and comes running back in.*

SCOTT. Sir…

MICHAEL (*the floodgates open*). I hate this, yes. But not because of what you write. I hate this because you don't know your value. You're really going to waltz in here and act like you've got the keys to the fucking kingdom.

And he's gesturing her to the door.

HEATHER. Who are you?

MICHAEL. Oh come on…

HEATHER. Who are you?

MICHAEL. This is just absurd.

HEATHER. Look at me and tell me you don't know.

Beat.

MICHAEL. What??

HEATHER. The book. He wrote a book. The *Observer* serialised it.

MICHAEL. Where's this going now?

HEATHER. A senior Party man was about to publish his memoirs. Rubbishing you. A story appears on the internet one day before: exposing him as having mental-health issues. (*And she's looking straight at* SCOTT. *Then back to* MICHAEL.) Tell me you didn't know. (*Beat.*) Tell me you're not interested in personalities.

MICHAEL. I didn't know. (*Beat.*) I didn't know.

HEATHER. The greatest crime in the media age. Is lying.

Pause. And then she packs up her things and goes.

Scene fades…

Scene Fifteen

MICHAEL *with his entourage – a gaggle of* ADVISERS. *Regular morning meeting – everyone packed in the room. Standing room only.*

ANTHONY *is now Chief of Staff* – SALLY*'s replacement. A rather smooth media executive with a very earnest style. Together they study the newspaper.*

MICHAEL. One week! Not even one week!

ANTHONY. Yes…

MICHAEL. What should be the defining moment of my premiership. Bringing the troops back home. Starts in less than a week.

ANTHONY. Sir…

MICHAEL. And you're telling me the moment has been hijacked!

Turns his attention, again, to the newspaper.

I rolled my tongue in my mouth.

ANTHONY. Says here you were stifling a yawn.

MICHAEL. I wasn't.

ANTHONY. *I'm* not saying you *were*. You weren't.

MICHAEL. Then we agree. Good-oh. So. Why are the knives out?

ANTHONY. Doesn't matter if you were or you weren't. There's a photo here with your mouth looking… odd. They're making an interpretation.

MICHAEL. People yawn.

ANTHONY. They do, yes. But not in front of the Cenotaph.

MICHAEL. I don't look at this stuff. I don't respond to profile pieces.

ANTHONY. I have to insist. I know it was Sally's office policy but now I'm Chief of Staff we must consider this. You've got a bored and bitchy media who see you pulling a face and suddenly – boom! You're yawning. At the grave of the unknown soldier. You're a man who doesn't give a fig about our troops.

SCOTT *laughs coldly. Thinks the word 'fig' is a funny choice.*

SCOTT (*explaining his mirth*). 'Fig.'

ANTHONY. Then there's the letter.

MICHAEL. Oh God, can we please…?

ANTHONY. No. I'm sorry. It's critical. We must discuss it. A letter signed by you, to the parents of a soldier who died. Boy's name misspelled in it.

MICHAEL. I was tired.

ANTHONY (*trying to ignore him*). The paper wheeled in a handwriting specialist – to analyse your signature. Just look.

Offers a copy. MICHAEL *takes it. It's* HEATHER*'s red-top paper.*

Says the writing style lacks… empathy. The shape of your vowels. Hurried. Uncaring.

MICHAEL. Bastards. (*Beat. Looks to* SCOTT *for a comment.*) How did they get hold of this?

SCOTT. Leak didn't come from the Party. Probably MoD. The letter – someone must have tipped them off.

MICHAEL. Ah.

ANTHONY. They think you're frivolous. They think you're not committed to a strong military. Complaining about the President's golf cart. They think you're a lightweight. That your heart isn't in it.

MICHAEL (*mounting anger*). My father…

ANTHONY. Mm.

MICHAEL. My father grew up without a mother.

ANTHONY. Sir.

MICHAEL. The Luftwaffe carpet-bombed Coventry. She went out one morning, the siren sounded. She never came back. And they think I don't know about that pain. (*Grabs the paper away from him.*) What do we do?

ANTHONY. Well – we don't make snap decisions. A period of consolidation, I'd say. We don't withdraw troops just yet.

MICHAEL. So. We're shaping policy based on what the papers say.

The silence that follows means 'Yes'. MICHAEL *is incandescent with rage. Papers fly.*

ANTHONY. Sir. *That* interview – I don't know what went on…

MICHAEL (*angry at himself*). I told her she 'didn't know her place'. I told her that she had no influence. Stopped short of calling her worthless. Actually, no, I probably said that too.

ANTHONY. Well, this is the fallout. A demonstration of power.

SCOTT. I'll prepare a statement for the house. We're committed to the war.

ANTHONY. Strongest possible language.

Beat.

MICHAEL. Because of a name. Spelled wrong.

Scene fades…

Scene Sixteen

MICHAEL *alone in his office.*

His phone buzzes. He puts it on speaker.

The voice at the other end of the line is his DIARY SECRETARY.

DIARY SECRETARY. Sir?

MICHAEL. Yes?

DIARY SECRETARY. I have her for you now.

MICHAEL. Yes.

DIARY SECRETARY. Okay. Go ahead please. Putting you through.

Phone clicks. And then a female voice comes on.

VOICE. Hello?

MICHAEL. Yes. This is Prime Minister Goodlad. Michael Goodlad. Thank you for taking my call.

VOICE. Yes?

MICHAEL. I just wanted to… actually… I wanted to speak to you and apologise. There's a lot been said in the press… how, when I wrote to you, I didn't really sympathise.

VOICE. Yes.

Beat.

MICHAEL. I have a daughter. Not too many years younger than your son. Once, a while back, we almost lost her. I know about that pain. I know about the pain of loss.

VOICE. Yes, sir.

MICHAEL. I made a mistake. I was tired. I was… preoccupied when I wrote you that note. Things have been busy here. Things have not been going all that well. It's not an excuse. But I was careless when I wrote that letter. I was feeling the pressure of office. (*Beat.*) Hello?

He can hear some strange sounds down the line – an odd clicking noise and then some chattering.

Is there someone else there with you?

Click. Click.

Jesus Christ. You're taping this conversation.

Scene fades…

Scene Seventeen

Early morning, orange sky.

MICHAEL *alone sifting papers.* SCOTT *knocks and enters. Looks dishevelled – clearly he has rushed to get here.*

MICHAEL. Just you? (*Beat.*) Where's Anthony?

SCOTT. I asked to see you on your own.

MICHAEL. I don't need you right now. Go. Please.

Beat. SCOTT *doesn't move.* MICHAEL *stares at him.*

SCOTT. You do. You need me. (*Beat. Shuts the door behind him.*) There's a splash in one of the tabloids. (*Has a copy of it – produces it.*) An exclusive, apparently. 'Goodlad comes apart on the telephone.'

MICHAEL. Bloody paper. Got her to tape me.

SCOTT. Yes.

MICHAEL. God knows how they persuaded her. Poor woman. (*Beat.*) The idea – the sheer offence of suggesting that I didn't feel…

SCOTT. You thought you'd give her a call.

MICHAEL. I did what I thought was right.

SCOTT (*gently at first*). There are rules. Golden rules. You never ever lose control.

MICHAEL (*irritated*). Obviously.

SCOTT. They have the last word. On everything. They always have the final right of reply. Not to mention editorial control. They can reshape your message – turn it into anything they like!

MICHAEL. I didn't actually…

SCOTT. You have offered them a juicy steak. With sauce! (*Reads the transcript.*) 'Sorry. It was a bad week. I was preoccupied.' A man coming apart. I should have known. I should have been handling this, not you.

MICHAEL. You're not the Prime Minister.

SCOTT. And that's a shame. 'Cause if I was…

MICHAEL. Don't you fucking dare…

SCOTT. YOU REALLY DIDN'T SMELL A SET-UP??

Beat.

MICHAEL. I don't know how one smells.

SCOTT. And I do. So there's a lesson there somewhere, Prime Minister.

MICHAEL. Don't ever…

SCOTT. 'To err is human.' Okay. Everyone makes a fluff from time to time. You spelled her son's name wrong on the letter. Slap on the wrist. Twitter storm. Dead story by teatime. But *with this* – this painful supplication – you have managed to keep the story alive. Comedians are doing jokes about it. Someone's mixed it into a dance track. Everyone's laughing! Everybody's laughing at me!!

MICHAEL. Well, I'm terribly sorry if your gleaming reputation has been dented, Scott, but actually – you know what? I've got rather bigger concerns than the fact that your hair has been ruffled.

SCOTT. Yes. Okay. Look…

MICHAEL. You do me a service, okay? You SERVE. You pick up the shit and you sweep up the mess. And you do it so I'M

FREE TO BE MYSELF. You're here to liberate me, not tie me up in fucking bandages.

SCOTT. Yes…

MICHAEL. They're laughing at you. Boohoo. The Party men who *so resented* me plucking you from the ranks. Now they're going to sneer. You feel humiliated. I'm so sorry. But that doesn't come into the equation. I hurt that poor woman. I insulted her son's memory. And I wanted to apologise. I'm not coming to you for permission – like I'm begging to be allowed out on a school night. (*Pause. Regains his composure.*) What do you want me to do? Tell me what you want me to do… and I'll do it.

SCOTT. It's fine.

MICHAEL (*sensing his discomfort*). Say it.

SCOTT. First time anyone's done a story about your press machine. (*Turns, looks at* MICHAEL.) Now they've got *me* in their gunsights. I'm no longer invisible. When the bloke in my job gets mentioned by name – his days are numbered.

Scene fades…

Scene Eighteen

Evening.

A formal reception is in progress – we can hear a military brass band downstairs in the hall playing the Armenian National Anthem. Eventually the music ends and there is applause from a large crowd.

Door opens and MICHAEL *enters, dressed formally, with* HEATHER *in a cocktail dress. The sound of lively chatter from scores of* GUESTS *blasting through the door.*

MICHAEL (*with gentle humour*). Bloody farce.

HEATHER. Oh dear.

MICHAEL. All that faffing just to take one photograph.

HEATHER. It did seem to be causing some problems.

MICHAEL. Two Prime Ministers and their wives. Shouldn't be that difficult. (*Reaches for a whiskey decanter and pours himself a drink.*) Wives in the middle looks wrong, they said. Makes us look like our spouses are running our countries.

HEATHER. Wives on the outside?

MICHAEL. Worse, apparently. Too much like a gay wedding. With lesbian ushers.

HEATHER *sniggers.*

And then there was the kiss, of course. Didn't help. Bloody European Heads of State. He really got in there and slobbered on me. I thought he might actually squeeze my bum. Never do business with a country if their flag has got orange in it.

He laughs it off and pours her a whiskey. Offers it.

HEATHER. Are we having drinks?

MICHAEL. Well, I'm drinking. So it seems polite to offer.

HEATHER. Symbolic drinks?

MICHAEL. 'Symbolic'?

HEATHER. Our last meeting… it was… I just wondered if… this was an olive branch.

MICHAEL. Um… I can pop an olive in it.

Beat. She takes the glass. They chink and drink.

HEATHER. Are you off-duty now?

MICHAEL. I've still got to make a speech. Swap gifts. Diplomacy, you know?

HEATHER. What are we giving them?

MICHAEL. Not a clue. I don't wrap them personally. (*Beat.*) Thanks for coming. Thanks for dressing up. Dinner should be decent. Stuffed trout. Just to say, I hope that…

HEATHER. …you hope a state dinner will put us back to where we were. Before…

MICHAEL. Yes. (*Beat.*) You're on the fun table.

HEATHER. Sir…

MICHAEL. Stephen Fry. And that woman who starred in *Broadchurch*…*

HEATHER. I need to say…

MICHAEL. Stuffed trout. Sauté of vegetables. Classic pud – lemon tart.

HEATHER. And after that you think we'll be okay?

He smiles: she looks unconvinced.

MICHAEL. I made an arse of myself. Thank God it was you. Thank God it was with a friend. All that stuff I heard myself say to you. How you don't matter. How you're irrelevant. Sometimes I get on a roll and start talking nonsense. 'The press doesn't know its value.'

HEATHER. You believe it. (*Breath.*) You still do.

MICHAEL. Please. Look. I want us to forget it.

She rummages in her bag, produces a document.

HEATHER. Tomorrow's editorial.

* hit ITV drama 2014/15 about the murder of a young boy + impact on the community. Stars David Tennant + Olivia Coleman

MICHAEL. Listen…

HEATHER. I thought I should let you see.

MICHAEL. Let me properly apologise…

HEATHER. Read it. (*Offers it but he won't take it.*) Okay, I'll read it. 'Government in meltdown.' Paper comes right out and says it.

Pause. The atmosphere is still oddly convivial. He speaks quietly, gently,

MICHAEL. If this is a joke… it's well executed.

HEATHER. It's not.

MICHAEL. You're coming out against me. Four months from an election. Sticking two fingers up.

HEATHER. Interesting. That's what bothers you most. My lack of deference.

Silence. He takes the article from her and reads it – every word. At that moment the military band strikes up downstairs. Still he is reading during the music. Then…

Am I still having dinner here?

MICHAEL (*glancing still at the article*). My my.

HEATHER. Yes.

MICHAEL. How many different ways can you call me 'weak'? How many ways can you call me 'feeble'? Truly… imaginative.

HEATHER. We had a thesaurus. Made good use of it.

He offers it back to her.

MICHAEL. You really think…?

HEATHER. No more off-the-record briefings. No more spin. And then you employed an assassin. Oh, I can see why you keep him – it's obvious. The lure of one's own professional villain. You think it makes you more secure, having him here. Truth is just the opposite. It's made your position untenable. You've fucked it.

MICHAEL *reins in his anger, finds his dignity.*

MICHAEL. I'll be judged by what I do in office.

HEATHER. Yeah, well, that's awkward 'cause nobody knows you at all. All they know is what I tell them. And I'm telling them you're an arrogant bastard. So.

Silence. He is trying to sit on a volcano of anger.

MICHAEL (*very softly*). I'll tell you what's arrogant… Arrogance is telling the world their damned opinion. Shoving it down their throats. Arrogance is making the fucking news. What happened to good old-fashioned reporting?

HEATHER. We tried that. You know what happened? We had to wait twenty-four hours to print every scoop. Twenty-four hours to get it in print and on the news-stands. Bastard bloody internet can do it in a minute and a half. Thatcher died – silly cow – mid-morning. We had to wait a whole day to publicise it. Yahoo had it up there in a matter of seconds. We're old. We can't compete. Solution? Fill the pages with opinions. Because that's all we can do. So, Prime Minister. That's my opinion of you.

Scene fades…

Scene Nineteen

MICHAEL *is meeting the* LEADER OF THE HOUSE OF COMMONS *– a distinguished woman in her forties.*

He spins on his chair – almost truculent – like a little kid, having a tantrum. She can't break through.

SCOTT *is here through the whole meeting, surfing on two phones simultaneously We get a sense that the whole operation is in his hands these days.*

LEADER. It's an issue of democracy.

MICHAEL. It's a pissing contest.

LEADER. Michael…

MICHAEL. It's a pissing contest. 'Who can pee the highest.' I'm not playing.

LEADER. Look – PMQ is sacred.

MICHAEL. I'm still turning up.

LEADER. You're shrinking the time away to nothing.

MICHAEL. It's a joust. Got nothing to do with questions. Got nothing to do with the answers I give. No one's listening to what I say. They just want to see me wriggle on a pin.

LEADER. It sends out the wrong message if you cancel.

MICHAEL. What message?

LEADER. Sir…

MICHAEL. What message does it send?

LEADER. You don't value the debate at all.

MICHAEL. But that's my message. Totally balls-on accurate. I don't value any of it!! I have fourteen researchers working flat-out the night before. It's not debate by any measure. It's just a test of how well I read their writing.

SCOTT *puts down his phones and wades in.*

SCOTT. The Prime Minister feels that there is very little to be achieved in subjecting himself to a jeering mob of infants.

LEADER. The Parliamentary Party.

SCOTT. Apes throwing faeces. This Prime Minister has work to do. Actual work. Houses to build. Anything else?

Beat.

LEADER. You're shirking.

MICHAEL *bursts out laughing.*

It's not just my opinion.

MICHAEL. *I'm a shirker??*

LEADER. There's gossip. In the tea room.

SCOTT. Ooh. Is there? For a change.

LEADER. Prime Minister's Questions are when you… set the tone. You lead.

MICHAEL. I take one for the team.

LEADER. People fear that…

MICHAEL (*unimpressed*). 'People'?

SCOTT. In the tea room!

MICHAEL. Too many backbenchers with too little to do. We need to instigate a work scheme. Get them all digging trenches. Anything to stop them gossiping.

LEADER. Look…

MICHAEL. Tea room is a morass of shit. Don't come to me with *the tea room.*

LEADER. What can I tell them? I'm Leader of the House. They come to me.

SCOTT. Tell them he's Prime Minister. AND THEY'RE NOT. END OF.

LEADER (*numbering on her fingers*). Hostile press and a discontented backbench. It's a downward spiral you can't control.

Silence.

MICHAEL. How many?

LEADER. What?

Beat.

MICHAEL. In the meeting. How many?

LEADER. There was no meeting.

MICHAEL. A groundswell. Of backbenchers. Asked to meet with you.

Beat.

LEADER. There was no meeting. (*Beat.*) There was no meeting. But there is an email. Doing the rounds.

MICHAEL. Ah yes, of course. Death by a thousand clicks.

Scene fades…

Scene Twenty

Very early in the morning.

MICHAEL *is on the phone – it's pressed to his ear and it's ringing. But no reply.*

ANTHONY *enters. Puts a mug of tea down in front of* MICHAEL.

MICHAEL. Not picking up. (*Hangs up.*) He's not picking up.

ANTHONY. Six thirty. It's early.

MICHAEL. We need a Whip count.

ANTHONY. Agreed. But not official. It'll make us look desperate.

MICHAEL. We need the Whips to take the temperature. (*Pause.*) Who's it going to be?

ANTHONY. Honestly? I don't know. I can take a guess.

MICHAEL. There's going to be a figurehead. Someone they can all line up behind. It'll be a resignation.

Knock on the door.

Aha. The politeness of my assassins.

DENIS *appears at the door.*

DENIS. Not too early, is it? Morning, Anthony.

ANTHONY. Mr Chairman.

MICHAEL. You brought a letter?

DENIS. Sorry?

MICHAEL. Nice of you to deliver it in person.

DENIS. Michael –

MICHAEL. Not a winner. Not the right man to lead us to victory. Am I anywhere close?

DENIS. Anthony, would you excuse us please?

ANTHONY. I'll be outside.

DENIS. Thank you.

And he's gone.

Twelve weeks.

MICHAEL. Yes.

DENIS. Thirteen points.

MICHAEL. You've done the maths.

DENIS. It's going to be like turning around a battleship.

MICHAEL. You think we can't do it.

DENIS. I think… it's going to be tough. The press has got it in for you. One paper in particular.

MICHAEL. She and I have an awkward… relationship.

DENIS. And now you're paying the price.

MICHAEL. Still. No use crying. You've come to tell me I'm a liability. Damaged goods. Shall we skip to the end?

DENIS. I'm telling you to fight. (*Beat.*) We need to repackage you. Remind everyone of your strengths. I can organise the workers. Rally the troops. I think you're still the right man for this. The last thing we need is a leadership contest. We need to fight the other side, not each other.

Beat. MICHAEL *is genuinely surprised.*

The alternative is surrendering to the media. Do you really want to give them that power? You were chosen by a democratic process. Let's not give in to them, Michael. Let's not allow them to be kingmakers. I've seen too many people… Good men. *Good men.* Prime Ministers that we deserved. People who would have been giants, stolen from us. How did we end up here?

MICHAEL. What do you propose?

DENIS. Sound the trumpets. Two hundred laptops – stick 'em in a warehouse. Get everyone onside. I'm looking forward to the fray. If you are too.

MICHAEL *stands tall.*

MICHAEL. Reckon I'm up for a fight. Rebellion is all about momentum. We slam on the brakes and – presto. We can win this thing.

DENIS. Good to see you're on the front foot. I'll call a council of war.

MICHAEL. Yup. A sit-down with all the key people.

And he's gone.

Next moment ANTHONY *pops his head around the door.*

ANTHONY. Sir? Have you got time for Ms Wells?

PRISCILLA *waltzes in through the door.*

MICHAEL. Just spoken with the Chairman. Feel quite buoyed.

She opens up her bag and takes out a letter.

What's that?

PRISCILLA. It's a letter. My… letter. Michael, I'm sorry. I've come here to resign.

Scene fades…

Scene Twenty-One

A council of war.

MICHAEL, ANTHONY, SCOTT, DENIS. *Four chairs drawn up at the table.*

ANTHONY. We're looking at sixty votes, I think.

DENIS. Sixty's do-able.

ANTHONY. She's got a fair wind behind her.

DENIS. We need to carve this list up. Stroke the talent. See all the rebels personally. You've still got a lot of support.

MICHAEL. Have you seen the letters coming in? (*Reads.*) 'Commiserations.' Always rely on your friends to tell you when they think you're finished.

A knock on the door. It's ELLIE.

ELLIE. Sorry. Sorry.

MICHAEL. No, it's fine.

ELLIE. Sorry to intrude.

DENIS. Eleanor.

ELLIE. Hi. (*Scuttles over to her dad with paperwork.*) Form you need to sign.

MICHAEL. Where's Mum?

ELLIE. Out. Sorry. Sorry. Urgent. Form for school. Needs doing.

MICHAEL. Okay. Give it. (*To the others.*) Do you mind?

He takes the form, starts to read it, pen poised.

ELLIE *hangs back. Glances once at* SCOTT. *Meets his gaze. She doesn't know him, even though he knows her.*

Carry on. Keep talking. I'm listening.

DENIS. We need a press strategy.

SCOTT. I've got her in my gunsights.

DENIS. Yes, look…

SCOTT. Got stuff in my back pocket. Tactical leaks. Spoilers. The whole playbook.

MICHAEL. Bloody right.

SCOTT. I've got… (*Chooses his words carefully –* ELLIE *is here, after all.*) favours I can call in. But our greatest asset is the gossip sites.

DENIS. Sir…

SCOTT. Make her wade in her own swill. Gossip will kill her.

DENIS. I think a cleaner approach is needed this time. (*Beat.*) Scott's approach. We're not sure if it's played well.

MICHAEL. 'We'?

DENIS. Anthony and I.

DENIS *is looking straight at* ANTHONY. *They have obviously discussed this prior to this meeting.*

SCOTT. Have I missed a meeting?

MICHAEL. We both have.

MICHAEL *gives* ELLIE *her form, nods for her to leave and she scuttles out.*

SCOTT (*dry*). You want me to step out of the room as well?

DENIS. Scott…

SCOTT. This is the Prime Minister's political survival. You want to bench me?

DENIS. There's a concern.

SCOTT. You think I'm part of the problem?

DENIS. Yes. Frankly. Yes, we do.

ANTHONY. It was effective at first, but I'm afraid that the Scott-brand has been tainted now.

A chilly pause.

Slurring your opponent. That stuff.

DENIS. It's common knowledge. Scott's name is in the paper too.

MICHAEL. It's in the paper because of me.

ANTHONY. That's immaterial.

MICHAEL. If he goes down then I go too.

ANTHONY. I disagree.

DENIS. He'll taint the whole campaign.

MICHAEL. If his methods are less than civil then.... our attackers are too. He... rescued us.

DENIS. And now that job is done.

ANTHONY. Is keeping Scott worth the office and the title?

SCOTT. You want me to resign!? 'Cause there's a risk I'll get mud on the carpet.

DENIS. Can we just talk seriously...?

SCOTT. Ditch the striker just before the final?

DENIS (*to* MICHAEL). I'm sorry. I must insist.

SCOTT. Ooh. Sounded like an ultimatum, that did.

ANTHONY. I'm with Denis. This is how it has to be.

SCOTT. Tag team.

DENIS (*to* SCOTT). I'd like to say 'It's not personal.'

SCOTT. But it is! (*To* MICHAEL.) I'll win this for you... You know I will.

DENIS. We have to fight her cleanly. (*To* MICHAEL.) I beg you – remember why you first got into office!!

SCOTT. Sir…

DENIS. This Party is a moral crusade.

SCOTT. Christ…

DENIS. …or it's nothing.

SCOTT. I'm the man for this.

DENIS. Remember what you said. WE CAN'T AFFORD TO THROW OUT WHO WE ARE JUST TO HANG ON TO THE THRONE.

Silence. MICHAEL *looks to* SCOTT *and back to* DENIS.

MICHAEL. You're saying I have choose, then. Yes?

Silence. Long silence. Seems to go on forever.

MICHAEL *opens his mouth, as if about to make his choice. Then…*

Scene fades…

Scene Twenty-Two

Next morning.

The STEWARDS *arrive and start to pack everything into boxes.* MICHAEL *is leaving Downing Street. Uniformed* MEN *and* WOMEN *wrap each ornament in bubble wrap and then place them all into cardboard boxes.*

MICHAEL *is wandering through the room, watching them as they work.* ANDREA *appears, arms filled with stuff she has collected. Both of them are dressed smartly.*

MICHAEL. Not sure where to go.

ANDREA (*shrugs*). Back up to the flat.

MICHAEL. There's stuff to do in here.

ANDREA. Leave it for the woman-with-the-wall-chart.

MICHAEL. There's a coup in Venezuela. Can't put it on hold until the music stops.

ANDREA. Send your calls upstairs. No point in you being here – not whilst they're dismantling.

MICHAEL. Steal something nice. Take everything that can't be nailed down.

She's on her way out, but he pulls her back. Takes her shoulders and kisses her.

ANDREA (*bit surprised*). What was that?

MICHAEL. I don't know. Just felt like it.

She is on her way again when she notices a Filofax lying on a desktop. Opens it up to check the name.

That's not mine.

ANDREA. No. It's Scott's.

It belonged to SCOTT. *For a moment it is as though* SCOTT *is back in the room*

What do you think he' s going to do with himself?

MICHAEL. Write a book, possibly. (*Beat.*) When they look him up in Wikipedia it's going to say he was a bastard.

ANDREA. Well, he *was* a bastard. But he can always change it. That's the beauty of it.

Beat.

MICHAEL. I should never have fired him. He was the last man standing in the trenches. My Praetorian Guard. I ought to write to him.

ANDREA. You can't.

MICHAEL. No. I just thought I would say it.

ANDREA (*goes to him, squeezes his arm*). This world you inhabit – I'm not sure that it makes for the best possible… men. Right from day one you're competing: doing hustings, or by-elections.

MICHAEL. You're right. It encourages bad... decisions. Fuelled by vanity most of the time.

ANDREA. Can't be easy staying yourself. You managed for a hell of a time.

MICHAEL. I could have stayed the course. I wavered. That's what killed me. I listened to the whispers one time and then... I couldn't stop listening. The moment you start to care what people are saying – you can't shut it out. I could have done more.

ANDREA. It's impossible not to listen.

One more kiss.

And then their daughter enters. She is dressed rather smartly for once.

MICHAEL. Hey.

ELLIE. I'm finding loads of stuff. Stuff that's been buried in cupboards since we got here. What are you doing?

MICHAEL. Being sad.

ELLIE. Really? I can't wait to get the hell out of here.

MICHAEL. Why are you dressed like that?

ELLIE. Same reason you are. Applause. And then photographs.

MICHAEL. Oh, no. You're not included.

ELLIE. Why not?

MICHAEL. Family rules. We'll scoot you out of the back door.

ELLIE. I dressed up specially. Put on a skirt and blouse – which you know I hate. I want to be seen coming out of Downing Street with my mum and dad. (*Breath.*) Going to stick my middle finger up.

ANDREA. Eleanor.

Beat. Then MICHAEL *and* ELLIE *laugh simultaneously. And then* ANDREA *sweeps away to finish her tidying.* ELLIE *looks out the front window. Pause.*

ELLIE. I thought I'd raise an army.

MICHAEL. What?

ELLIE. Ride up Whitehall. Lay siege outside the new King's door. It's what the eldest child does. I've been watching *Game of Thrones*. Job for the firstborn. (*Beat.*) Bollocks to them. (*Beat.*) Can I say that?

MICHAEL. Yep. I'm fine with 'bollocks'. (*Breath.*) Can say 'Fuck 'em' if you want.

ELLIE. Fuck 'em. (*Beat.*) I've got your back.

She smiles. He smiles. And then quite suddenly his eyes well up with tears. ELLIE *is embarrassed when she sees his embarrassment – the room is still full of* STEWARDS.

She offers him a crumpled tissue from her cardigan pocket.

You want me to go?

MICHAEL. No. We're leaving together.

ANDREA *enters the room, beckons to them.*

ANDREA. Come on.

And they leave side by side.

Scene fades.

The End.

* epic book series + hit TV adaptation (Sky TV)
- extreme violence + sex

A Nick Hern Book

Feed the Beast first published in Great Britain as a paperback original in 2015 by Nick Hern Books Limited, The Glasshouse, 49a Goldhawk Road, London W12 8QP, in association with Birmingham Repertory Theatre and New Wolsey Theatre, Ipswich

Cover image by New Wolsey Theatre

Designed and typeset by Nick Hern Books, London
Printed and bound in Great Britain by Mimeo Ltd, Huntingdon, Cambridgeshire PE29 6XX

A CIP catalogue record for this book is available from the British Library

ISBN 978 1 84842 483 8